CITYSPOTS
PALMA

Teresa Fisher

C000122278

Written by Teresa Fisher
Updated by Sally Davies & Nadia Feddo

Published by Thomas Cook Publishing
A division of Thomas Cook Tour Operations Limited
Company registration No: 1450464 England
The Thomas Cook Business Park, 9 Coningsby Road
Peterborough PE3 8SB, United Kingdom
Email: books@thomascook.com, Tel: +44 (0)1733 416477
www.thomascookpublishing.com

Produced by The Content Works Ltd
Aston Court, Kingsmead Business Park, Frederick Place
High Wycombe, Bucks HP11 1LA
www.thecontentworks.com

Series design based on an original concept by Studio 183 Limited

ISBN: 978-1-84157- 874-3

First edition © 2006 Thomas Cook Publishing
This second edition © 2008 Thomas Cook Publishing
Text © Thomas Cook Publishing
Maps © Thomas Cook Publishing/PCGraphics (UK) Limited
Transport map © EMT

Series Editor: Kelly Anne Pipes
Production: Steven Collins

Printed and bound in Spain by GraphyCems

Cover photography (Llotja, Palma de Mallorca) © Marco Cristofori/zefa/Corbis

CONTENTS

SYMBOLS KEY

The following symbols are used throughout this book:

ⓐ address ☎ telephone ⓦ website address ⓛ opening times
ⓝ public transport connections ❶ important

The following symbols are used on the maps:

𝑖	information office	▨	points of interest
✈	airport	O	city
✚	hospital	O	large town
⛊	police station	○	small town
▣	bus station	══	motorway
▤	railway station	—	main road
✝	cathedral	—	minor road
❶	numbers denote featured	—	railway
	cafés & restaurants		

Hotels and restaurants are graded by approximate price as follows:
£ budget price ££ mid-range price £££ expensive

Abbreviations used in addresses:

Avda.	Avinguda (Avenue)
C/.	Carrer (Street)
Pl.	Plaça (Square)

◗ View of Palma and its marina

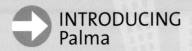

INTRODUCING
Palma

Introduction

Palma Town, beautifully situated at the centre of Palma Bay, is the capital of the Balearic Islands. This vibrant, cosmopolitan city has managed to retain a great deal of its ancient charm. Its street life and thriving arts scene lead many people to compare it with the stylish Catalan capital, Barcelona. Indeed, many people also feel that Palma is the best place to live in all of Spain – because of its chic shops and avant-garde galleries, its thriving pavement café society, excellent restaurants and lively nightlife and, above all, because of its sheer vitality, and the flair and enthusiasm of its inhabitants.

The most striking image of Palma is its triumphant cathedral (see page 66), standing proud on the waterfront and almost seeming to grow out of the sea. Fanning out behind the cathedral is the Old Town and Arab quarter, a warren of narrow lanes shielding ancient palaces and mansions, with elegant courtyards featuring stone stairways and potted plants. A short stroll from here leads to Plaça Major, a pleasant square of open-air cafés, at the heart of the pedestrianised shopping district with its many small speciality shops. Amble down leafy La Rambla, with its dozens of flower-sellers, through Plaça Weyler and Plaça del Mercat with their unusual *Modernista* (art nouveau) architecture, tree-lined Passeig des Born, the city's main promenade since the early 15th century, and into the narrow maze of streets around Sa Llotja – venue of some of the smartest hotels, bars and restaurants in town. From here it is a stone's throw to the waterfront, where the real lifeblood of Palma lies. Fishermen mend their nets, cruise ships sail into the harbour, and the designer bars along the Passeig Marítim buzz with conversation after dark.

There's no denying Palma offers both residents and visitors the good life and – with the opening of new shops, galleries, hotels and restaurants – the future looks bright. Long overlooked, it is finally becoming a popular holiday destination in its own right. Easy access makes it perfect for a weekend away. Seek out its many treasures, soak up its cosmopolitan atmosphere, and you will discover the true Palma – laid-back, vibrant and one of the most exhilarating cities in Spain.

● *The Rambla is one of the city's most pleasant streets*

When to go

There is no wrong time to visit Mallorca, but bear in mind that while winter is much quieter, many tourist-oriented hotels, restaurants and so on, close for extended periods. Conversely, in July and August you will find that many shops and offices will be closed.

SEASONS & CLIMATE

Palma's temperate climate makes it a pleasant city break destination all year round. However, when planning your holiday you may wish to consider the old Mallorcan saying, *Hasta el cuarenta de mayo no te quites el sayo*, meaning 'Don't discard your coat until the 40th day of May' (in other words, until 10 June), which is considered to be the first day of summer.

Most people choose to visit between April and September, when the island is invariably warm and sunny. July and August are the

● *Palma's year-round sunshine is one of its greatest assets*

hottest months, when temperatures can rise well above 30°C (86°F). However, Palma is also popular at other times of the year, and usually more pleasant for a city break outside the sweltering summer high season. During January and February, the almond blossom makes an unforgettable sight, and Easter is especially popular, with its mild spring days. However, autumn is generally regarded as the best time to visit, when the main tourist rush is over but the sea is still warm enough for bathing and the evenings remain balmy enough for al fresco dining. During the winter, many beach resorts and tourist facilities around the island close down, but Palma continues to attract visitors all year round. Its wettest months are generally October and February. In the depths of winter temperatures in the city can drop as low as 2–3°C (35–7°F), while snow occasionally falls in the mountains in the north of the island.

ANNUAL EVENTS

Fiestas and festivals are an integral part of Mallorcan life. The inspiration for most festivities is religious, and *Semana Santa* (Holy Week, the week leading up to – but not including – Easter Sunday) plays an especially important part in the city's cultural calendar. The fiesta season is at its busiest between June and September.

January & February

Fiesta of Sant Sebastià Flamboyant parades, processions, fireworks at the port and city-wide celebrations honour the patron saint of Palma. 🕐 14–20 Jan

Cavalcades Sa Rua (Carnival Parades) As the austerity of Lent approaches, the Palmesanos erupt in a riot of last-minute extravagance, with feel-good carnivals and no-holds-barred fun. 🕐 31 Jan–5 Feb 2008; 18–24 Feb 2009

March & April

Semana Santa Holy Week sets off a host of celebrations and processions: on Palm Sunday, the Processions of Hooded Brotherhoods see penitents marching around La Rambla de los Ducs de Palma de Mallorca; on Maundy Thursday, an image of the crucified Christ is carried through the city. 🕐 16–22 Mar 2008; 5–11 Apr 2009

July

Día de la Virgen de Carmen Parades take place in the city and fishing boats are blessed in honour of the Virgin Mary. 🕐 15–16 July

October

Fiesta of Santa Catalina Tomas Singing, processions and entertainment enliven the city's streets. 🕐 Third Sun

🔺 *Dramatic firework displays mark the Fiesta of Sant Sebastià*

December

Noche Buena Christmas is marked with Nativity plays and midnight mass services. 🕑 24 Dec

Festa de l'Estandard A festival commemorating the Catalan conquest of the island in 1229 segues into a New Year knees up. 🕑 31 Dec

---

PUBLIC HOLIDAYS

As well as countless local festivals and fiestas, many Spanish national holidays are observed in Palma. The main ones are:

New Year's Day 1 January

Epiphany 6 January

Balearics Day 1 March

Maundy Thursday 20 March 2008; 9 April 2009

Good Friday 21 March 2008; 10 April 2009

Easter Monday 24 March 2008; 13 April 2009

Labour Day 1 May

Assumption of the Virgin 15 August

National Day 12 October

Todos los Santos (All Saints' Day) 1 November

Constitution Day 6 December

Feast of the Immaculate Conception 8 December

Christmas Day 25 December

Boxing Day 26 December

On national holidays, most businesses and shops are closed, public transport is reduced to a minimum, and it can be difficult to find accommodation. At Easter and Christmas many shops and offices are closed for longer periods.

Palma's art & architecture

Mallorca has long been an artists' haven, thanks to its Mediterranean location, its exotic blend of European and Arabic culture, and its beautiful landscapes. Modern art, in particular, has flourished since the start of the 20th century, thanks largely to two men, the great Catalan artist, Joan Miró (1893–1983), and the great Catalan architect Antoni Gaudí (1852–1926).

ARCHITECTURAL GENIUS

In 1902, a local bishop, having seen Gaudí's flamboyant Sagrada Família church in his home town of Barcelona, invited him to restore Palma's cathedral. Gaudí spent ten years working intermittently on the cathedral, introducing to Palma Europe's latest architectural fashion, *Modernista*, or Spanish art nouveau – a trend known to some as *la época de mal gusto* ('the epoch of bad taste'). He made some radical changes to the interior of the cathedral, including the introduction of electric lighting, wrought-iron railings and a highly controversial canopy symbolising the Crown of Thorns, made from cardboard, cork, brocade and nails. (This was just a model – hence the cardboard. The real thing was never constructed, due to financial constraints.) Gaudí's influence can be seen in several of Palma's early 20th-century buildings, including Pensió Menorquina (see page 66) in Plaça del Mercat, with its rippling façades.

AN ARTISTIC 'SAINT'

Joan Miró's arrival in Mallorca also boosted artistic creativity throughout the island. Both his mother and wife were Mallorca-born and the great painter and sculptor spent his childhood holidays and the last 40 years of his life living and working on the outskirts of Palma in

🔺 *Elaborate ironwork is a trademark of the* Modernista *style*

Cala Major. He frequently remarked how his boyhood observation of the ever-changing Mallorcan sky, with its shooting stars and lazy fireflies – one assumes that the relative lack of pollution in those days made star-gazing particularly rewarding – inspired him and planted the creative seeds that ultimately flowered in his work.

During his time in Mallorca, Miró moved away from realism and developed his own characteristically spontaneous style of bold lines and bright splashes of primary colours. His studio in Cala Major remains almost untouched since his death, as part of the Fundació Pilar i Joan Miró (see page 107), and, to Mallorcans, he is nothing less than a saint.

History

Mallorca abounds in ancient monuments dating back to the earliest traces of civilisation here in 5000 BC. From caves to stone-built houses, the Talayotic civilisation followed around 2000 BC and, largely due to their strategic location in the Mediterranean, the Balearic Islands soon became important trading posts for Phoenicians, then Greeks and Carthaginians, who used the islands for piracy. At this time, the locals were known for their ability to defend themselves by using slings, hence the archipelago received its name, derived from the Greek word *ballein*, meaning 'to throw from a sling'.

Mallorca flourished under the Romans (123 BC–AD 500), with the introduction of Christianity, vines and olives, and a network of roads and settlements – including two major cities, Palmaria (Palma) and Pollentia (Pollença). After successive invasions by the Vandals and the Byzantines, the island eventually fell to the Arabs in 902. Moorish culture prevailed for several centuries. Oranges, windmills, new irrigation techniques, almonds and apricots were introduced, and the lifestyle of citizens in Palma (then known as Medina Mayurqa) was the envy of Europe, with their heated baths, street lights and covered sewers. This sophistication drew the attention of potential conquerors, and in 1229 the young Catalan king, Jaume I of Aragón, set sail to conquer the 'pirates' nest of Mallorca'. He seized Palma – 'the most beautiful city I have set eyes upon' – on New Year's Eve, and proceeded to replace the mosques with churches and to build the imposing Castell de Bellver. His reign (1229–76) is still regarded as Mallorca's golden age of independence.

Despite centuries of relentless invasions and conquests, by the start of the 14th century Palma was considered to have one of the most economically successful societies in Christendom. Its merchants' palaces were much admired and the Mallorcan cogs were the best ships on the sea, leading the way in Atlantic exploration. The island's cartographers became celebrated throughout the world. Following a period of political uncertainty in the 16th century, sea trade started to flourish again in the 18th and 19th centuries and, in 1833, a regular ferry service enhanced links between Palma and mainland Spain.

The island's seafaring tradition continued into the early 20th century, bringing visitors by yacht or on cruise ships to Palma. But it wasn't until 1950, with the arrival of the first charter flights, that Mallorca witnessed the birth of package tourism. Almost overnight the island became one of Europe's most popular holiday destinations, as greedy developers bulldozed their way along the coast around Palma, eager to cash in on the enormous economic potential of their beaches, in an uncontrolled building boom. Palma, however, has always been more than a developers' playground. In the past five years, it has restored its palaces and museums and shed its image of dusty provincialism. Every week another chic new shop opens, or a boutique hotel, a trendy bar or a minimalist restaurant. Yet at the same time, Palma maintains a careful balance between traditional and modern. Finally this vibrant, cosmopolitan city has now become a popular holiday destination in its own right.

⬤ *Junipero Serra, Mallorcan founder of California*

Lifestyle

The population of Mallorca is around 790,000, of whom nearly half live in Palma. The islanders are loyal, friendly and fiercely proud of their identity. They are a largely conformist society, centred on the family and the church – the Catholic Church has held sway here since Jaume I's reconquest in 1229. Mealtimes are an especially important occasion, when friends and family gather together. Mallorcans love to spend time over their dinner. They enjoy good lively conversation and never rush their food. They eat hugely but always drink in moderation – unlike many of the foreign visitors holidaying on the island, you never see an islander drunk.

The pace of life in Palma is lively compared with the rural interior. The city is the economic, political and commercial capital of the island, and although the Palmesanos work hard, they play hard, too. Office hours (typically 08.00–13.00 and 16.00–19.00) fit neatly around a lengthy afternoon siesta, giving locals the energy to party late into

● *Fishing is a great stress-buster for some Mallorcans*

WHAT'S IN A NAME?

The Palmesanos refer to Palma simply as Ciutat ('City') – a reference to its first name, Civitas (Latin for 'city'), given by the Romans who also called the city Palmaria. It wasn't until the 16th century that it was called Palma – a shortened version of the Roman name. In between, it became known as Medin (Arabic for 'city'), and later, when the Christians seized the city, it was called Ciutat de Mallorca. Oh, and by the way, 'Mallorca' is the Mallorquín version of the English 'Majorca'. Clear?

the night. For a true taste of Palma, chat to locals over early-morning coffee and *ensaimadas* (sweet pastries) in a simple café; shop till you drop with the smart set in Avinguda Sant Jaume III – the cost of living is generally higher in Palma than elsewhere on the island; then join in their evening *paseo* (a ritual evening stroll when all the family parade their best clothes) down the Born and along Passeig Marítim as the sun sets over the Bay of Palma.

Visitors to Palma will hear a variety of languages in the streets – many of its inhabitants are foreigners, especially during summer months. Most Mallorcans are bilingual, speaking both Castilian Spanish and a local version of Catalan known as Mallorquín. During the Franco regime, Mallorquín was banned, but it is once again recognised and can be heard throughout the island, although Catalan is acknowledged as the 'official' language. Numerous ex-pats live in the city, and so British and other foreign-language newspapers and magazines can be bought from newsagents in the city centre and in some of the larger resorts, including the popular English-language newspaper *Majorca Daily Bulletin*, affectionately known as 'The Daily Bee'.

Culture

Palma has long been the main cultural hub of the Balearic Islands, famed for its enormous number of outstanding buildings, monuments and art galleries. However, in recent years, its reputation has stretched further afield, and it is now considered to be an important Mediterranean cultural centre, known particularly for its modern art and its prestigious musical events.

Visitors to Palma can enjoy concerts and music festivals throughout the year, including a festival of classical and light music for the Sant Sebastià fiesta in January, an international week of organ music in March, a spring opera season from March to June at the Teatre Principal (see page 79), a series of 'summer serenades' in the Castell de Bellver (see page 86) throughout July and August, as well as festivals and concerts throughout the summer months, and a week of organ performances in October. Then there's a winter series of concerts by the Ciutat de Palma Symphony Orchestra.

Palma wears its history on its streets, with its eclectic mix of architecture. The buildings of Palma bear witness to over a thousand years of history, from the Royal Palace of Almudaina (Palau Reial de l'Almudaina, see page 62), built by Muslim rulers and remodelled by Christian kings, to La Seu (see page 66) – one of the world's finest Gothic cathedrals – and the city's immaculately restored merchants' palaces. Some of these are still owned by the descendants of the wealthy patricians who built them, and occasionally they open their doors to the public, providing a rare glimpse of bygone life during Palma's maritime heyday. Otherwise, the city's fascinating museums leave no stone unturned, ranging from the ancient remains of the

● *Enigmatic sculpture at the Fundació Miró*

Arab Baths (see page 58) to the ultra-modern new gallery, Es Baluard (see page 87) – a riot of glass, metal and brick, built inside an ancient city fortress overlooking the Bay of Palma.

Mallorca has long attracted painters and there are more than 50 private galleries in Palma that exhibit works mainly by Mallorcan and Catalan artists. Several hold regular free exhibitions of contemporary art, ranging from conventional landscape scenes to avant-garde abstract works by such leading local exponents as Miquel Barcelo. The island's public foundations also help to promote local culture, funding free exhibitions of visual arts in such venues as Fundació La Caixa (see page 69), Ca'n Solleric (see page 88), Sa Llotja (see page 80) and Fundació Juan March (see page 69). Art appreciation is currently in vogue in Palma, and a handful of galleries have recently opened cafés, bars and bookshops on their premises to attract a wider audience.

Tourists, too, can really get to know and love this culturally rich city by participating in the popular series of daytime guided walks on such themes as 'The City and the Sea', 'Modernism in Palma', 'Monumental Palma', 'The Jewish Quarter' and, an evening stroll entitled 'The Stories and Legends of Palma'. Contact the tourist office (see page 152) or call ❶ (971) 720720 for information.

❶ *A luxury yacht cruises into Palma*

Shopping

Palma is without doubt the best place to shop in Mallorca. The main shopping district lies within the old city walls and can easily be explored on foot. As Palma's confidence has grown over the past few years, so has its shopping scene increased (and, regrettably, its prices). Growing numbers of chic boutiques and design shops have opened in the city centre – taking their lead from their trendy Catalan neighbour, Barcelona, less than four hours away by ferry – putting Palma on the map for even the most indefatigable shopaholic.

Serious shoppers should head for Avinguda Jaume III, long considered the city's most exclusive shopping boulevard, lined with designer boutiques, and Palma's main branch of Spain's leading department store, El Corte Inglés (see pages 72 and 90). Those who enjoy browsing in small, specialist shops should make for the area around Plaça Major. Carrer de Jaume II and pedestrianised Carrer de Sant Miquel are good for reasonably priced boutiques, Carrer de Sindicat abounds with shoe shops, and Carrer de l'Argentería is best for jewellery – look out for Mallorca pearls.

Some of the most fascinating shops are hidden away in the narrow streets and alleyways of the Old Town, where you can find such genuine Mallorcan articles as carved olive-wood, hand-blown glass and glazed earthenware pots painted with the Spanish symbols of cockerels or flowers. Look out also for *siurell* (clay whistles) in the shape of a man on a donkey, rope-soled espadrilles, and authentic lace and cotton decorated with the traditional Mallorcan *llengua* (tongue) pattern.

For self-catering visitors, there is an excellent choice of well-stocked supermarkets but, for fresh produce, you can't beat the

Olivar market hall (🅐 near Plaça d'Espanya 🕒 every morning except Sun) for fruit, vegetables, meat and cheese. A big *rastrillo* (flea market) takes place on Saturday mornings in Avinguda Villalonga.

Most shops open Monday to Friday from 09.00 or 10.00 until 13.00, when they close in the afternoon for a siesta, reopening around 16.30 until 20.00 or even later during summer months. On Saturdays, shops only open in the morning. However, hypermarkets stay open all day, and El Corte Inglés (see pages 72 and 90) is open Monday to Saturday from 10.00 until 22.00.

USEFUL SHOPPING PHRASES

What time do the shops open/close?
¿A qué hora abren/cierran las tiendas?
¿A kay ora abren/theeyerran las teeyendas?

How much is this?
¿Cuánto vale?
¿Cwantoe baleh?

Can I try this on?
¿Puedo probarme esto?
¿Pwedo probarme esto?

My size is ...
Mi número es el ...
Mee noomairo es el ...

I'll take this one, thank you
Me llevo éste, gracias
Meh llievo esteh, gratheeas

This is too large/too small/too expensive. Do you have any others?
Es muy grande/muy pequeño/muy caro. ¿Tienen otros?
Es mooy grandeh/mooy pekenio/mooy karo. ¿Teeyenen ohtross?

Eating & drinking

Palma's impressive range of restaurants suits every taste and budget from pizza to paella, and from gourmet cuisine to Chinese takeaway. The growth in tourism over the past few decades has led to an increasing number of international restaurants in Palma. Traditional Mallorcan cuisine, however, is typically Mediterranean, making full use of local produce – especially pork, fish and vegetables – all heavily flavoured with garlic, tomato and herbs.

Most meals start with bread and olives (often the tart green olives typical of the island), followed by fresh leafy salads in summer and hearty broths for chilly winter days. Popular local dishes include *frito mallorquín*, a fry-up of liver, potatoes and tomatoes, and *sopes mallorquines*, a thick vegetable soup containing slices of brown bread, as well as the delicious *tumbet*, a ratatouille of potatoes, peppers and aubergines. The Mallorcans are hearty meat-eaters – charcoal grills are a speciality, along with roast suckling pig and shoulder of lamb. *Sobrassada* sausages, made by mincing raw pork with hot red peppers, can be seen hanging in butcher's shops and tapas bars,

PRICE CATEGORIES

In this book the approximate price bands into which restaurants fall are based on the average cost of a three-course evening meal for one person, excluding drinks, indicated by these symbols:

£ up to €25   ££ €25–40   £££ over €40

Bear in mind that a one-course lunch in a £££ establishment may well be at a ££ cost, and so on.

🔺 *What better place to dine?*

along with whole cured hams. Seafood features on most menus and there is a glut of fish restaurants, especially on the waterfront. Lobster, prawns and sardines are always excellent, and sea bass baked in rock salt is an island speciality.

The classic Spanish dish is, of course, paella – a mound of steaming rice flavoured with saffron and topped with everything from mussels and prawns to pieces of chicken. The Mallorcan equivalent is *arròs brut* ('dirty rice'), which uses chicken and pork but no seafood. Paella is available in all of Palma's fish restaurants and in many of the resorts, but be wary of anyone who says they can serve it immediately – if cooked properly it takes at least 20 minutes to produce.

Tapas bars abound in Palma, and the area around Plaça Llotja is especially popular. These Spanish nibbles are designed to whet the appetite before a meal, but order enough of them and they'll make a meal on their own. They are usually lined up in a display cabinet beneath the bar in metal trays, so it is easy to choose what you want by pointing. Typical tapas range from plates of ham, cheese and olives to more exotic offerings such as fried squid rings, garlic snails, stuffed peppers and meatballs in tomato sauce.

For a simple lunchtime snack, try *pa amb oli*, an open sandwich consisting of thick brown bread rubbed with tomato and olive oil, and topped with ham or cheese. Another popular snack is *tortilla*, a delicious potato omelette which is sometimes served cold. Most bars serve *bocadillos* (filled rolls), and bakeries are a good place for stocking up on picnic provisions. Look out for *coca* (a kind of thin, crunchy pizza), *empanadas* (small pasties filled with meat, fish or spinach) and *ensaimadas* (spiral-shaped pastries that can be either savoury or sweet). Add cheese, fruit and vegetables from the covered market, Mercat del Olivar (see page 75), and your picnic is ready to enjoy in a city park or at the beach.

The *vino de la casa* (house wine) in most restaurants will probably be Mallorcan and is frequently excellent, though most places will also stock a selection from mainland Spain. *Cava*, or Spanish champagne, makes an inexpensive treat and can be combined with orange juice for a refreshing cocktail. Beer (*cerveza*) is usually lager, sold draught or bottled. (If you want draught, ask for *una caña*.) Sherry, which is normally a dry *fino*, served chilled, is the perfect drink to accompany a plate of ham before a meal. Another refreshing drink is *sangria*, an alcoholic fruit punch based on red wine, brandy and lemonade – delicious, but beware, it's more potent than it tastes. Most bars stock a good selection of Spanish brandies – popular brands include Soberano and Fundador – but, for a truly local drink, try *hierbas*, a herb-based Mallorcan liqueur which comes either sweet or dry.

Most Mallorcans eat their main meal at lunchtime, and tend to eat dinner late in the evening. Some restaurants do not take reservations, but in summer it's advisable to book for dinner if possible, especially if you're planning to eat in an expensive or popular restaurant. At the end of the meal, it is normal to leave a tip of ten per cent, assuming service is not included.

USEFUL DINING PHRASES

I would like a table for ... people
Quisiera una mesa para ... personas
Keyseeyera oona mesa para ... personas

May I have the bill, please?
¿Podría traerme la cuenta, por favor?
¿Podreea tryairme la cwenta, por fabor?

Waiter/waitress!
Camarero/Camarera!
¡Camareroe/Camarera!

Could I have it well-cooked/medium/rare please?
¿Por favor, la carne bien hecha/al punto/poco hecha?
¿Por fabor, la kahrneh beeyen etcha/al poontoh/poko etcha?

I am a vegetarian. Does this contain meat?
Soy vegetariano. ¿Tiene carne este plato?
Soy behetahreeahnoh. ¿Teeyeneh carneh esteh plahtoh?

Where is the toilet (restroom) please?
¿Dónde están los servicios, por favor?
¿Dondeh estan los serbeetheeos, por fabor?

Entertainment & nightlife

Palmesanos certainly know how to enjoy their evening entertainment and nightlife. Indeed, local artist Santiago Rusinyol once famously remarked, 'The people of Palma take the moon as others take the sun'. It's true – Palma is a city that never sleeps. A typical evening might begin with tapas in a local bar after work with friends or colleagues, followed by dinner late in the evening. Theatre performances rarely start before 22.00, cinemas frequently have late-night showings, and the pavement terraces of bars and cafés are usually bustling with activity well into the early hours on summer evenings, while the nightclubs party till dawn.

Palma boasts Mallorca's widest range of entertainment, attracting world-class performers year round. On the cultural front, there are three main theatre venues staging everything from classical to contemporary drama (most performances are in Spanish) as well as dance, ballet, classical concerts, opera and *zarzuela* (Spanish light opera). There are also several cinema complexes in the city, showing mostly 'original version' movies subtitled in Castilian Spanish. Programmes are advertised in the local newspapers. Each venue has its own box office.

Perhaps the most popular evening pastime, however, is people-watching at a pavement terrace, while sipping a chilled beer, a bottle of local wine or a *café con hielo* (coffee with ice) with friends. The main core of the city's nightlife is in the city centre, along the waterfront and especially in the maze of ancient side streets behind Plaça Llotja. Here you will find bars to suit all tastes, budgets and ages from trendy neon-lit cocktail bars, to more traditional-style cafés, even pubs and dark smoky blues bars, some of which stay open until dawn.

There is also a wide variety of live music, from mellow jazz to flamboyant displays of authentic flamenco *sevillanas* and *rocieros*, or simply just a good old singsong in an Irish bar. Near the cathedral, Ses Voltes (see page 79) in the Parc de la Mar is a popular open-air venue for live pop, rock or jazz bands most weekends. The city also has a vibrant busking scene, from classical musicians performing around the cathedral square, to human 'statues', clowns and folk bands along La Rambla and the Passeig des Born.

After midnight, night owls should head west along the Passeig Marítim for the currently 'in' late-night bars on the Darsena de Ca'n Barbara, before rubbing shoulders with the likes of the Crown Prince of Spain, Michael Douglas and Claudia Schiffer in the hippest nightclubs in town. There are plenty of clubs to choose from, with DJs playing everything from house and hip-hop to chart sounds and Latin beats.

Although Palma's nightlife is thriving, it is currently fashionable for the chic set to head out of town to the sophisticated bars of nearby Porto Portals, Mallorca's very own St Tropez, a short distance along the coast to the west, or to the smart new waterfront bars and cafés of Portixol, a trendy suburb to the east of Palma.

To find out what's on when, check out the listings on the tourist office's official website ⓦ www.infomallorca.net, or pick up a *Mallorca Week* events sheet, produced in English from the tourist office. The English-language newspaper, the *Majorca Daily Bulletin* (available at most news kiosks and online at ⓦ www.majorcadailybulletin.es), provides a guide to what's on in the Balearics. There is also a free monthly island guide in English called *Digame*, detailing Mallorcan cinema, theatre, art, music and nightlife available in selected bars and cafés and hotels (and online at ⓦ www.digame-online.com).

Sport & relaxation

SPECTATOR SPORTS

Mallorcans are football crazy, and the island's two main teams – **Real Mallorca** (Ⓦ www.rcdmallorca.es) and **Atlético Baleares** (Ⓦ www.atbaleares.com) – are both based in Palma, with regular matches from September to April.

Horse-racing is another great day out. The sport has been popular here for over 200 years, ever since neighbouring villages used to race each other during fiestas. Trotting races take place every Sunday at the **Son Pardo Hippodrome** (ⓐ Carretera Palma-Sóller, Km 3 ⓘ (971) 754031 Ⓦ www.hipodromsonpardo.com).

Bullfighting is not as popular as in mainland Spain, but the city's bullring is the third-largest in the country and holds fights on selected Sundays between March and October (ⓐ Pl. de Braus, Av. Arquitecte Gaspar Bennàzar 32 ⓘ (971) 755245).

🔺 *Golf is increasingly popular and well catered for*

Sailing is a spectacular spectator sport, with regattas in Palma Bay including the Princess Sofia Trophy in April and the Copa del Rey in August – both major international yachting events patronised by King Juan Carlos.

PARTICIPATION SPORTS

The range of participatory sports available in Palma is wide and the facilities excellent. Watersports are popular, with small boats, canoes and pedalos for hire on the Platja de Palma (Palma Beach) at Can Pastilla and S'Arenal. There is a scuba-diving club in Palma, **Isurus Club** (ⓐ C/. Magalhaes 8 ⓣ (971) 730943 ⓦ www.isurussub.com) and jet-ski hire from the **Club Náutico** at S'Arenal from June to September (ⓐ Paseo Cala Gamba ⓣ (678) 652080 ⓦ www.cnarenal.com). For details on water-skiing, contact the **Escuela Esquí Náutico** (ⓐ C/. D. Rafael Pablo, Hotel Bonanza Playa, Illetes ⓣ (971) 702024).

In recent years, golf has boomed. The best of Mallorca's 18 courses are just a stone's throw from Palma, and include **Real Golf de Bendinat** (ⓣ (971) 405200 ⓦ www.realgolfbendinat.com) near Illetas, and **Golf Son Muntaner** (ⓣ (971) 783030 ⓦ www.sonmuntanergolf.com) and the exclusive **Son Vida** (ⓣ (971) 791120 ⓦ www.sonvidagolf.com), located just northwest of the city in a lush area of countryside known as S'Hort de Palma (the Garden of Palma).

RELAXATION

Walkers, cyclists and nature-lovers should leave the city and head for the mountains, where the huge variety of terrain and the abundance of flora and fauna have a mighty chill-out factor. To scale the big peaks, it is best to join a guided trek organised by the **Federacíon Española de Deportes de Montaña y Escalada** in Palma (ⓣ (971) 468807 ⓦ www.fedme.es).

Accommodation

Palma offers visitors an excellent choice of accommodation, with over 50 hotels ranging from top-class international chains and ultra-chic boutique hotels to simple hotels and inexpensive hostels for travellers on a budget. Surprisingly, there are no campsites on Mallorca.

Hotels are classified by government inspectors with a star system that goes from the basic 1-star to 5-star luxury. Prices are regulated by the tourist authorities and breakfast is usually not included, unless you are on a package holiday. Tariffs are displayed at the reception desk and in individual rooms. A tax of seven per cent (rising to 15 per cent in 5-star hotels) may or may not be included in the quoted price of your hotel, so it is always advisable to ask prior to booking. The amount is always specified on the rate card.

If you are without transport, stay in the heart of the city, in a converted palace in one of the narrow streets of the medieval centre, or in the alleys behind Plaça Llotja, where the bulk of Palma's budget accommodation can be found, as well as some of its fanciest boutique hotels. For a room with a view, consider a hotel on the Passeig Marítim overlooking the harbour, and, for unadulterated luxury, choose one of the 5-star deluxe hotels on the outskirts of the city.

PRICE CATEGORIES
The ratings below (unrelated to the official star system) indicate the approximate cost of a room for two people for one night (excluding VAT and breakfast):
£ up to €100   ££ €100–200   £££ over €200

Wherever you stay, early booking is essential, especially during high season. You are unlikely to find vacancies by simply walking around the city. It is always advisable to book in advance, either directly with the hotel or through a central booking system, such as the **Central de Reservas de la Federación Empresarial Hotelera de Mallorca (FEHM)** (🕾 (971) 706007 🌐 www.mallorcahotelguide.com).

HOTELS

Pons £ A simple, 1-star hotel in a beautiful old house, with rooms arranged around a central courtyard. 🅰 C/. Vi 8 🕾 (971) 722658

Ritzi £ The clean, simple rooms in this popular, British-run, 1-star hotel are ideal for the budget-conscious traveller. 🅰 C/. Apuntadores 6 🕾 (971) 714610 🌐 www.hostalritzi.com

Azul Playa ££ Opened in 2007, the Azul Playa is a modern hotel in Ciutat Jardí, out beyond Portitxol. It has 17 rooms, some of which look out over the sea, and all of which have a terrace. 🅰 C/. Isla de Rodes 24 🕾 (971) 919020 🌐 www.hotelazulplaya.com

Dalt Murada ££ A stylish, family-owned, 15th-century town house with tapestries and chandeliers, in a deserted backstreet near the cathedral: rooms are arranged around a sunny courtyard of orange and lemon trees. 🅰 C/. Almudaina 6a 🕾 (971) 425300 🌐 www.daltmurada.com

Misión de San Miguel ££ A chic new boutique hotel tucked down an alleyway near the Plaça Espanya. The rooms are comfortable, if minimalist in style, and the best are those that look out over the central courtyard. 🅰 C/. Can Maçanet 1 🕾 (971) 213848 🌐 www.hotelmisiondesanmiguel.com

Palau Sa Font ££ Just off the Passeig Marítim and near the main nightlife area, this charming 16th-century episcopal palace has been transformed into a small, bijou hotel, combining traditional materials with modern Mediterranean décor. ⓐ C/. Apuntadores 38 ⓘ (971) 712277 Ⓦ www.palausafont.com

⬤ *The Palau Sa Font was once the bishop's residence*

Palladium ££ Centrally located and a short walk from the Old Town, this comfortable, 3-star hotel is a popular business choice. ⓐ Passeig de Mallorca 40 ⓣ (971) 712841 ⓦ www.hotelpalladium.com

San Lorenzo ££ An elegant baroque mansion full of Mallorcan character in the old fishing quarter, with just six rooms, a picturesque garden and a small, outdoor pool. ⓐ C/. San Lorenzo 14 ⓣ (971) 728200 ⓦ www.hotelsanlorenzo.com

Almudaina £££ A moderately sized 3-star hotel in the city centre, on Palma's fashionable main shopping precinct. Ask for a room with a view over the rooftops to Palma Bay. ⓐ Avda. Jaume III 9 ⓣ (971) 727340 ⓦ www.hotelalmudaina.com

Arabella Sheraton Golf Hotel £££ Arguably the island's most luxurious hotel, with its own Michelin-starred restaurant, Plat d'Or, a relaxing spa and acres of mature gardens adjoining a prestigious golf club, five km (three miles) north of the city. ⓐ C/. de la Vinagrella s/n ⓣ (971) 787100 ⓦ www.sheraton.com

Born £££ A former 16th-century *palacio* in the old city, this has been tastefully converted into a simple, comfortable 2-star hotel. ⓐ C/. Sant Jaume 3 ⓣ (971) 712942 ⓦ www.hotelborn.com

Convent de la Missió £££ An ultra-modern 4-star hotel in a converted monastery near La Rambla, with spartan white interiors, a Zen-inspired rooftop terrace and a whirlpool and sauna in the ancient crypt. ⓐ C/. de la Missió 7a ⓣ (971) 227347 ⓦ www.conventdelamissio.com

Costa Azul £££ A high-rise hotel on the seafront that is centrally located and excellent value, if a little noisy. There is a swimming pool and each room has its own balcony overlooking the bay.
ⓐ Passeig Marítim 7 ⓣ (971) 731940 ⓦ www.hotelcostaazul.es

Palau Ca Sa Galesa £££ Palma's most exclusive hideaway – a sumptuous, 17th-century *palacio* at the heart of the medieval city, crammed with antiques and artworks by Calder and Miró.
ⓐ C/. Miramar 8 ⓣ (971) 715400 ⓦ www.palaciocasagalesa.com

Portixol £££ This sophisticated seafront hotel, a ten-minute walk from the city centre on the revamped Portixol Marina, caters to a young, jet-set crowd. ⓐ C/. Sirena 27 ⓣ (971) 271800 ⓦ www.portixol.com

Puro Oasis Urbano £££ Palma's funkiest hotel is ideal for a hedonistic getaway weekend. Its 24 white rooms with jellybean-coloured accents smack of Ibizan hippie-chic, and its cool clientele lounge either in the rooftop hot-tub or in the sophisticated after-hours bar.
ⓐ C/. Montenegro 12 ⓣ (971) 425450 ⓦ www.purohotel.com

Tres £££ One of the latest boutique hotels to open in Palma, this hip joint in the Old Town has 41 comfortable, designer rooms, a beautiful courtyard, a sauna and a rooftop terrace with breathtaking views of the cathedral. ⓐ C/. Apuntadores 3 ⓣ (971) 717333 ⓦ www.hoteltres.com

YOUTH HOSTEL

Albergue Juvenil Platja de Palma £ One of just two youth hostels on the island, about 20 minutes out of town, and only open in high season (February to October). It is frequently block-booked by school groups.
ⓐ Costa Brava 13 ⓣ (971) 260892 ⓦ www.turismejove.com ⓝ Bus: 15, 23

🔺 *You can find some small seaside hotels dotted around the bays*

THE BEST OF PALMA

Palma is relatively small, compact and easy to explore on foot, with its leafy promenades, maze of ancient streets, stepped alleyways and sun-soaked squares flanked by ageing mansions and magnificent palaces. Most of the main city sights lie within the Old Town and along the seafront. Apart from one or two excursions to the outskirts and neighbouring resorts, there is little need to stray beyond the ancient boundaries of the Old Town. (Attractions of special appeal to families with children are described on pages 148–150.)

TOP 10 ATTRACTIONS

- **La Seu** A mighty sandstone cathedral that's undoubtedly the jewel in Palma's crown (see page 66)

- **Palau Reial de l'Almudaina** An ancient palace that bears witness to centuries of conflict between the Moors and the Christians (see page 62)

- **The Seafront & Port** Everything from tiny traditional fishing boats to super-yachts, naval vessels and massive cruise liners (see page 83)

🔻 *The architecture of the Palau March could be termed surreal*

- **Es Baluard, Museum d'Art Modern i Contemporani** Palma's newest museum contains a formidable collection of modern art (see page 87)

- **Castell de Bellver** The only circular castle in Spain, with a truly *bell ver* (beautiful view) of Palma Bay from its rooftop (see page 86)

- **Palau March** A stunning collection of modern sculpture, alongside some fascinating temporary exhibitions (see page 70)

- **Basilica de Sant Francesc** The tranquil cloisters here provide respite from the crowded alleys of the Old Town (see page 61)

- **Plaça del Mercat and Plaça Weyler** Admire the *joie de vivre* of the *Modernista* architecture here (see page 65)

- **Fundació Pilar i Joan Miró** The museum and studio of the island's greatest 'adopted' artist (see page 107)

- **Mountain train to Sóller** The vintage train ride through the Mallorcan countryside to Sóller is a journey not to be missed (see page 128)

Suggested itineraries

HALF-DAY: PALMA IN A HURRY

If you only have a few hours, start at the Parc de la Mar (see page 62), where the magnificent golden sandstone cathedral, La Seu (see page 66), is reflected perfectly in the lake. Climb the steps of the medieval walls and visit the interior of the cathedral, then explore the old Arab quarter – a warren of medieval streets where the wealthy Catalan merchants built their palaces during the city's maritime heyday. Pop into the Museu de Mallorca (see page 70) – with a grasp of the island's colourful history, walks around town are all the more rewarding. Grab a coffee in a locals' bar, before returning for a tour of the Almudaina. Then relax in the old royal

● *Get some serious shopping done while in Palma*

gardens, S'Hort del Rei (see page 61), with their shady orange trees, fountains and modern sculptures.

1 DAY: TIME TO SEE A LITTLE MORE

After you have done the recommended half-day sightseeing, add some shopping to your itinerary: stroll along the tree-lined boulevards of Passeig des Born and La Rambla, and explore the craft shops and boutiques in the streets around Plaça Major. Alternatively, take in an art gallery: Es Baluard (see page 87) is a must to see the local Impressionist paintings of the island, and it also has a wonderful terrace café overlooking the bay for light refreshment. At the end of the day, enjoy some al fresco tapas in one of the bars of Plaça Llotja, before exploring the maze of tiny lanes and alleyways behind the square, whose myriad restaurants, bars and clubs ensure an excellent evening out.

2–3 DAYS: TIME TO SEE MUCH MORE

The extra days give you plenty of time to explore the waterfront. The best image of Palma is from the sea, so take a boat trip round the bay, or stroll along the Passeig Marítim past fishing boats, yachts and Mediterranean motor cruisers, until you reach the westernmost part of the port with its naval vessels and huge cruise liners. There are some well-placed cafés en route. You may also have enough time to hop on a bus to Castell de Bellver, to the caves at Gènova or to Cala Major to see the Fundació Pilar i Joan Miró (see page 107).

LONGER: ENJOYING PALMA TO THE FULL

A longer stay enables you to soak up the café culture of the Old Town, to top up your tan on the beaches in the Badia de Palma, and to check out some of the city's vibrant late-night clubs and bars. You should also take at least one trip out of town (see page 113).

Something for nothing

Palma is the perfect destination for budget travellers, as there are plenty of sights and attractions to amuse you, without the need to spend a single euro.

For a taste of ancient Palma, explore the old historic centre – a picturesque maze of narrow streets and stepped alleyways fanning out around the cathedral (see page 66), with hidden, fountain-filled squares, ornate churches and beautifully restored mansions. Peer into their elegant courtyards with their flower-bedecked patios and arcaded balconies. Look out also for the amazing statues and carvings throughout the city, from the celebrated *Sling Thower* in S'Hort del Rei (the King's Gardens, see page 61) to the finials of the Ajuntament (Town Hall, see page 58). For a taste of local colour, join the residents of Palma window-shopping in Avinguda Jaume III and stroll along the seafront for yet more historic sights and fantastic viewpoints.

If all that walking sounds too energetic, soak up the atmosphere in the city squares, or pass a few hours watching street performers in Plaça Major and in the leafy boulevards of El Born and La Rambla, where you will find everything from buskers and magicians to human statues. Alternatively, escape the city bustle and people-watch on the floral terraces of the **Jardines de Sa Faixina** (❸ junction of Avinguda Argentina & Passeig Marìtim); or take a book, find a shady seat and drift off to sleep to the soothing sound of the gently splashing pools and fountains in the old royal gardens, the Hort del Rei (see page 61).

Even art aficionados on a tight budget need not be disappointed, as Palma boasts several galleries with free entry, including Ses Voltes (see page 79), Sa Llotja (see page 80), Fundació La Caixa (see page 69) and Ca'n Solleric (see page 88). Ask the tourist office for details of their exhibitions.

⬤ *The atmospheric Basilica de Sant Francesc cloisters cost nothing to enjoy*

If you're lucky, you may even experience one of Palma's 'free' parties, should your visit coincide with one of their big fiestas, when city-dwellers take to the streets in fancy dress in enormous parades, with brass bands, floats and fireworks.

When it rains

The good news is that it rarely rains in Palma. When it does, don't despair! The city has plenty of attractions to cheer up the dullest, wettest day.

For starters, the city abounds in museums and galleries to suit all interests. Immerse yourself in history at the Arab Baths (see page 58), the Museu Diocesà (see page 69) or the Museu de Mallorca (see page 70). Visit one of numerous art galleries, or pause a while in the city's magnificent churches. The Basílica de Sant Francesc (see page 61) is best known for its beautiful cloisters, while La Seu, the 'Cathedral of Light' (see page 66), is one of the largest and most beautiful Gothic cathedrals in the world (and an all-weather must-see). An ideal way of travelling from sight to sight is on the open-top hop-on-hop-off Sightseeing Bus (see page 56). Obviously you wouldn't want to sit upstairs if it's raining, but there's always plenty of room on the lower floor.

If the rain persists head to one of the large shopping centres – Porto Pi (see page 108) on the seafront, or Festival Park (see page 103) for factory outlet shopping and family fun just outside town – or to the cinema. Most complexes show original-version movies, subtitled in Castilian Spanish.

Better still, do as the locals and pass the time in the countless cafés and bars. There's always an excuse to nip in for a drink, whether it's coffee and *churros* (fried batter sticks) for breakfast, a quick, mid-morning espresso pick-me-up, tapas and *tertulia* (a chat with friends) for lunch or an early-evening get-together with friends for a *copa* (a quick sherry, liqueur or cognac) before dinner. You could even sample several bars in one evening, by following the Andalusian custom of the *tapeo*, moving from bar to bar just sampling one tapas dish in each. *Buen apetito!*

⬤ *Cool and peaceful, and dry when it's raining – the Arab Baths*

On arrival

TIME DIFFERENCE
Like the rest of Spain, Mallorca follows Central European Time (CET), which is one hour ahead of Greenwich Mean Time (GMT+1).

ARRIVING
By air
Son Sant Joan Airport (❶ (971) 789000), Palma's only international airport, is located 10 km (6 miles) east of the city centre and is easily accessible from all parts of the island. The high-tech, modern terminal is one of the busiest in Europe during summer months, and has excellent facilities, including 24-hour first-aid services and a post office in the Check-in area (second floor), a pharmacy and a bank in Departures (fourth floor) and several cash dispensers and exchange

🔺 *A spot of sun-worship eases the rigours of air travel*

booths in arrivals (ground floor). Other services include VIP lounges, and a good selection of shops, bars and restaurants, including a 24-hour bar and a 24-hour cafeteria. There is no left-luggage facility and the lost property office is situated in arrivals on the ground floor. Airport information desks (❶ (971) 225000) can be found in arrivals, Departures and at Check-in, and there is a tourist information desk on the ground floor (❶ (971) 789556). Car hire desks are located in arrivals and include such companies as Avis, Europcar and Hertz (see page 56).

If you're not hiring a car, a taxi into Palma (from outside Door 4 on the arrivals level) will take approximately 15 minutes and cost around €15. Alternatively, bus 1 runs from the airport to Plaça d'Espanya in Palma city centre approximately every 15 minutes from 06.10 until 01.10. The journey takes around 30 minutes and costs €1.85. There is a bus stop outside Door 4 of the arrivals area and another in front of the multi-storey car park.

By rail

Mallorca's main train station is located at Plaça d'Espanya in Palma. A narrow-gauge railway runs from Palma to Inca, Sa Pobla and Manacor. The journey lasts about 50 minutes. An old wooden train runs to Palma from the mountain town of Sóller, and takes about 55 minutes. The resort of Port de Sóller on the northern coast is a short ride to Sóller by an equally old wooden tram. Phone ❶ (971) 752245 (Inca-Manacor) and ❶ (971) 752051 (Sóller) for information.

By road

Mallorca's main bus terminal is located at Plaça d'Espanya in the city centre. An efficient bus network connects all the main towns in Mallorca to Palma. Phone ❶ (971) 176970 for information.

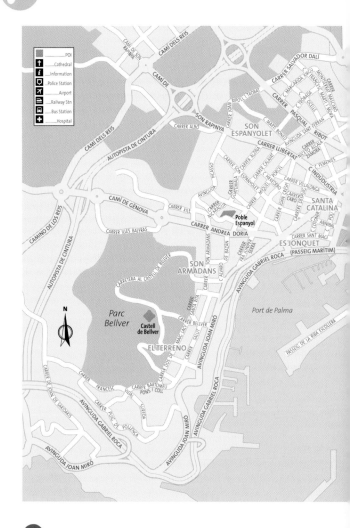

Palma

0 — 250 metres

0 — 250 yards

Driving in Mallorca is relatively straightforward, and it is easy to access all parts of Palma from the Via Cintura (ring road), which is clearly signed from the airport. Remember to drive on the right and stick to the speed limits: 120 km/h (74 miles/h) on motorways, 100 km/h (62 miles/h) on main roads, 90 km/h (56 miles/h) on other roads, except in urban areas, where it is 60 km/h (37 miles/h) unless otherwise signposted.

If you are planning to drive in Palma, invest in a detailed street map and familiarise yourself with the main streets in advance. Although main sights are clearly signposted, there are several one-way systems that can be confusing. Parking can also be difficult. Public car parks are expensive and it is virtually impossible to find a vacant place in the streets. Your best bet is to find a parking lot marked in blue with a *Zona Blava* (Blue Zone) sign, and to purchase a ticket (valid for a maximum of 90 minutes, depending on the area) from a nearby parking meter. Tickets are generally required on weekdays 09.00–13.00 and 17.00–20.00, and on Saturdays 09.00–13.00. Failing that, the most popular underground car parks are by the cathedral, Plaça Major and Plaça Espanya, so be prepared to queue.

FINDING YOUR FEET

On first impression, Palma appears to be a bustling Mediterranean city, but the pace of life here is surprisingly relaxed. The people are laid-back, friendly and happy to help tourists, and many of them speak English. It is also a safe city with a low crime rate. However, it is advisable to take the normal precautions you would in any city. Don't carry excess cash, and use the hotel safe for valuable goods; don't leave anything visible in a parked car; beware of pickpockets in crowded places; don't leave valuables on the beach or poolside, and stick to well-lit, populated areas by night.

ORIENTATION

Palma is compact enough to explore easily on foot, though very occasionally it's more efficient to use public transport. The city divides into two distinct areas: the Old Town surrounding the cathedral and city centre, to the east of the Passeig des Born, and the main nightlife area, to the west of the Passeig des Born, including the harbour and promenade area, called the Passeig Marítim. The ancient maze of side streets can be confusing, so familiarise yourself with the main avenues in the city centre –

IF YOU GET LOST, TRY ...

Excuse me, do you speak English?
Perdone, ¿habla usted inglés?
Perdoneh, ¿ahbla oosted eengless?

Excuse me, is this the right way to the Old Town/the city centre/the tourist office/ the station/the bus station?
Perdone, ¿por aquí se va al casco antiguo/al centro de la ciudad/a la oficina de turísmo/a la estación de trenes/a la estación de autobuses?
Perdoneh, ¿por akee seh ba al kasko anteegwo/al thentroe dey la theeooodad/a la offeetheena dey toorismoe/a la estatheeon dey treness/a la estatheeon dey owtoebooses?

Can you point to it on my map?
¿Puede señalármelo en el mapa?
¿Pwaydeh senyalarmayloe en el mapa?

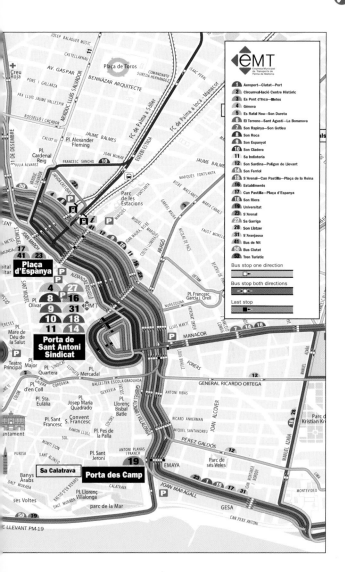

La Rambla dels Ducs de Palma de Mallorca (normally known as 'La Rambla'), Carrer de l'Unio, Avinguda Jaume III and Passeig des Born – which interconnect and split the capital neatly into two. Should you get lost, use such unmissable landmarks as the cathedral and the Bay of Palma to get your bearings.

The maps in this book show all the main streets and sights, but for further exploring, invest in a detailed street map, obtainable anywhere in Palma.

GETTING AROUND

The bus network is excellent and links the capital to most places on the island. It is also the best way to visit the city suburbs. All buses pass through the main bus station in Plaça d'Espanya and route maps can be found at every bus stop and at the tourist information office. The driver is paid on entering, so have small change ready,

● *A horse and carriage offer tours around Palma*

and keep your ticket for inspection. The *Tarjeta 10* scheme offers books of 10 bus tickets for €8 and is available from most tobacconists – useful if you intend to use the bus frequently.

The **Palma City Sightseeing Bus** is a good way to get your bearings. It leaves every 20 minutes from various stops around the city, and you can hop on and off at 16 stops (otherwise the round trip takes about 75 minutes) at the main city sights (Ⓦ www.city-sightseeing.com). Tickets are €13 and valid for 24 hours.

White taxis are an expensive option. A green roof light marked *Lliure* or *Libre* indicates they are available for hire. *Galeras* (horse-drawn carriages) are an alternative choice for sightseeing in Palma. There are ranks beside the cathedral and the Passeig de Sagrera, with a list of fares. Or hire a bicycle from **Ciclos Bimont** (ⓐ Pl. Progrés 19 ⓣ (971) 731866 Ⓦ www.bimont.com) and enjoy the 5 km (3 mile) cycle lane along the seafront.

CAR HIRE

It is only worthwhile hiring a car if you are heading out of town to explore the island. There are several hire car companies at the airport, although pre-booking via your airline's affiliates should secure you reduced rates.

Avis ⓐ Passeig Marítim 16 ⓣ (971) 286233 ⓐ Aeropuerto ⓣ (971) 789187 Ⓦ www.avis.es

Europcar ⓐ Passeig Marítim 19 ⓣ (971) 737589 ⓐ Aeropuerto ⓣ (971) 789135 Ⓦ www.europcar.es

Hertz ⓐ Passeig Marítim 13 ⓣ (971) 734737 ⓐ Aeropuerto ⓣ (971) 789670 Ⓦ www.hertz.es

---

❶ *You can see virtually the whole of the city from Castell de Bellver*

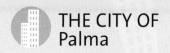

THE CITY OF
Palma

Eastern Central Palma

To the east of the city's main thoroughfare, the Passeig des Born, lies the historic centre of Palma. Here you will find the very essence of Mallorca's capital city – the magnificent cathedral (see page 66) overlooking a harbour of mega-yachts; cobbled streets leading to hidden, sun-drenched squares flanked by ancient palaces and exuberant churches; avant-garde art galleries; leafy promenades; *Modernista* architecture, superb shopping, and an excellent choice of pavement cafés, restaurants and tapas bars. What's more, the district is small and compact, and easy to explore on foot.

SIGHTS & ATTRACTIONS

Ajuntament

Palma's imposing 17th-century town hall is not actually open to the public, but should you pass it when the grand main doors are open, peek inside and you will catch a glimpse of the *gigantones*, folkloric 'giants' that parade the streets whenever Palma has a fiesta. Join locals relaxing on the stone benches surrounding this impressive building, and be sure to gaze skywards to see the unusual wood carvings overhanging the façade. They are the work of a naval carpenter, which is why they look more like the figureheads of ships than traditional finials. ❸ Pl. Cort ❶ (971) 225900 ⓦ www.palmademallorca.es

Banys Arabs (Arab Baths)

The ornate columns and elegant domes of these baths, dating from the tenth century, are one of the few surviving monuments from Mallorca's long period of Moorish rule. From 902 until 1229 there was a Moorish city, the Medina Mayurqa, here. The baths were

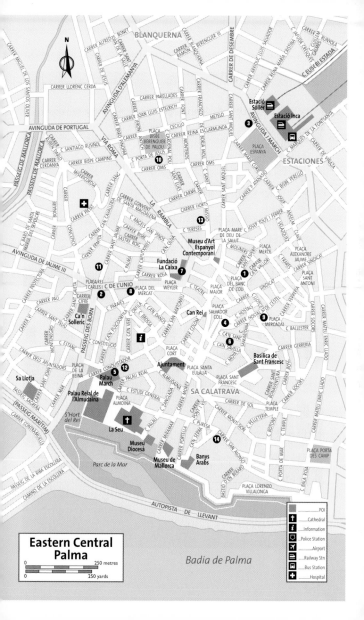

Eastern Central Palma

0	250 metres
0	250 yards

Badia de Palma

	POI
	Cathedral
	Information
	Police Station
	Airport
	Railway Stn
	Bus Station
	Hospital

originally part of a palace belonging to an Arab nobleman. Built in Roman style, they were used as health spas and meeting places. Bathers would move between the hot, steamy *caldarium* and the cooler *tepidarium*, before cooling off in the courtyard. Today the fountain-splashed garden is still a delightful place to relax, with its cacti, palms and citrus trees. ⓐ C/. Serra 7 ⓣ (971) 721549 ⓛ 09.30–19.00 Apr–Nov; 09.00–18.00 Dec–Mar. Admission charge

Basilica de Sant Francesc (Basilica of St Francis)

Visit this impressive Gothic church and you will be greeted outside by a statue of Friar Junípero Serra, the Mallorcan Franciscan friar who, during a pilgrimage to America, became one of the founding fathers of what is now California. The sober façade belies a surprisingly ornate interior, with lavish side chapels and an exuberant high altarpiece. But the pièce de resistance here is undoubtedly the adjoining 14th-century cloister, with its central fountain dating from 1638 and pointed archways, which give the cloister an almost Moorish feel. Shaded by lemon trees, the cloister has been declared a national monument and is a veritable oasis of peace. ⓐ Pl. Sant Francesc 7 ⓣ (971) 712695 ⓦ www.franciscanostor.org ⓛ Church 09.30–10.00, 18.00–20.00; cloister 09.30–12.30, 15.30–18.00 Mon–Fri, closed Sat & Sun. Admission charge

S'Hort del Rei (The King's Garden)

Escape from the hustle and bustle of the city and enjoy an afternoon siesta amid the flowers, fountains and statues in this cool, fragrant garden at the foot of the Palau de l'Almudaina. Look out for the celebrated *honderos* statue (see page 68) and also Joan Miró's *Egg*.

ⓞ *Make for the cloisters of the Basilica de Sant Francesc for some peace and quiet*

This sculpture marks the start of the tourist office's walking tours of the city (see page 20), and also the hop-on-hop-off open-top bus tours (see page 56). ⓐ Avda. Antonio Maura

Palau Reial de l'Almudaina

Palma's magnificent Royal Palace seems to rise out of the city walls on the seafront beside the cathedral. There has been a palace here since the Muslim governors built their *alcázar* (or fortress) soon after the Arab conquest, and before that a Roman fortress. Although it was later converted into Gothic style, some elements of Islamic architecture remain, including the loggia and the Arc de la Drassana Reial, the entrance to the royal shipyards that once stood alongside the palace. The *almudaina* (meaning 'citadel') later became the residence of the kings of Mallorca, and it is still the official residence of the Spanish royal family today. Visits are by guided tour only, starting in the central courtyard, and take in the Chapel of Santa Ana, the palace museum and the state apartments. ⓐ C/. Palau Reial s/n ⓣ (971) 214134 ⓦ www.patrimonionacional.es/almudain/almudain ⓛ 10.00–13.15, 16.00–17.15 Mon–Fri, 10.00–13.15 Sat, Oct–Mar; 10.00–17.45 Mon–Fri, 10.00–13.15 Sat, Apr–Sept. Admission charge

Parc de la Mar

The mighty city walls, the cathedral and the Palau Reial de l'Almudaina (see above) provide a striking backdrop for this large seafront park, built in the 1960s on land reclaimed from the sea. With its palm-shaded terraces, superb children's playground and outdoor cafés, it is one of the capital's most popular outdoor spaces to relax in all year round. What's more, it also provides the

---

ⓞ *The magnificent Palau Reial de l'Almudaina*

most photogenic views of the cathedral, perfectly reflected in its beautiful ornamental lake.

Plaça Major

This long, arcaded square at the heart of a busy shopping district is especially popular for its pavement cafés, street entertainment and artisans' stalls, and makes an ideal place to pause during a shopping spree. The square was built in the early 1800s, surrounded by four-storey, apricot-coloured buildings with green shutters, and with an arched portico on the ground floor containing a wide variety of shops. The city's main fish and vegetable market was here until the 1950s, when it was relocated to its larger site (Mercat del Olivar, see page 75) nearby. Beneath the square are a shopping centre and underground car park, where remains of a fortified Moorish wall were discovered during excavation work. But it's the local shopping that is the main crowd-puller here; narrow, labyrinthine streets lead off in all directions from the square, each one packed with boutiques and craft shops.

Plaça del Mercat & Plaça Weyler

These bustling squares contain some of the capital's most dazzling architecture. Plaça Weyler boasts Palma's first *Modernista* building – the ornamental Gran Hotel, constructed by the Catalan architect Lluis Domènech i Montaner in 1903, and magnificently restored. Today it contains the Fundació La Caixa (see page 69). Opposite, the Forn des Teatre bakery is probably the city's most photographed shop, with its attractive green and yellow *Modernista* décor. The adjoining leafy square of Plaça del Mercat contains two further

◀ *One of Palma's most photographed sights is in the Plaça del Mercat*

Modernista buildings – Pensió Menorquina and Edifici Casasayas, commissioned in 1908 by wealthy Palma resident Josep Casasayas, but their façades are relatively sober examples of the style. The square also contains a statue of the island's most famous politician, Antoni Maura (several times prime minister of Spain at the start of the 20th century), and the Palau de Justicia, Palma's courthouse.

La Rambla

La Rambla (Rambla dels Ducs de Palma de Mallorca, to be precise) has been one of the city's main promenades for many years. Once the main watercourse through the city, today this impressive tree-lined avenue is filled with the colourful stalls of Palma's daily flower market.

La Seu (Cathedral)

Palma's marvellous Gothic cathedral occupies a prominent position overlooking the harbour at the edge of the old city. For centuries it has been the symbol of Palma and a welcome sight to home-bound sailors, standing proudly out on the city's skyline.

It is said that when Jaume I set sail to conquer Mallorca from the Moors in 1229, he vowed to build a cathedral large enough to reach the sky if his mission succeeded. The result was this remarkable 'Cathedral of Light', one of the largest and most beautiful Gothic cathedrals in the world, and an expression of his political power – strategically built on the seafront for all to see, on the site of the former Great Mosque.

The foundation stone for the cathedral was laid by Jaume in 1230, but it has been extensively remodelled over the years and

▶ *Palma's La Seu must be one of the best-sited cathedrals in the world*

THE SLING THROWER

The Balearic archipelago is thought to have taken its name from the Greek word *ballein* meaning 'to throw', and a statue in S'Hort del Rei commemorates Mallorca's famous *honderos* (fighters with slingshots), who defended the island from attack.

was not completed until 1601. As a consequence the exterior, built from local golden *Santanyí* sandstone, demonstrates a variety of architectural styles, although Gothic predominates, with its massive flying buttresses, turrets and pinnacles.

The interior is most striking for its sheer proportions. The central nave alone is 121 m (400 ft) long and is supported by 20 m- (66 ft-) high pencil-thin pillars. The stained-glass windows are impressive too, especially the huge 15th-century one above the presbytery. Much of the interior was modified at the start of the 20th century by the famous Catalan architect Antoni Gaudí (see page 12), who worked here over a period of years, adding electric lighting and constructing the enormous canopy which hangs over the high altar, symbolising the Crown of Thorns. The cathedral is entered through the northern door, where alms were dispensed to the poor. ❸ Pl. Almoina, s/n ❶ (971) 723130 ❼ www.catedraldemallorca.org ❹ 10.00–18.15 Mon–Fri, 10.00–14.15 Sat, closed Sun (except during High Mass). Admission charge

CULTURE

Palma prides itself on being a city of art and culture and many of its major museums and galleries can be found in the Old Town. Some of the museums are housed in beautifully restored Renaissance *palacios*, and one gallery is contained within the former Gran Hotel (see page 65), one of the city's finest *Modernista* buildings, with its impressive, restored façade.

Can Rei

The intricate coloured façade of mosaics and its ornate wrought-ironwork make this house the finest *Modernista* building in Mallorca. Built by a local silversmith, Lluis Fortesa Rei, it shows strong influences of Gaudí (see page 12). ⓐ C/. Bosseria

Fundació La Caixa

This art gallery in the former Gran Hotel (see page 65) has a permanent exhibition of Mallorcan paintings, as well as changing temporary displays, and a popular art bookshop. The building itself, a fine example of Catalan *Modernista* architecture, is also worth a look.
ⓐ Pl. Weyler 3 ⓣ (971) 178500 ⓦ www.fundacio1.lacaixa.es
ⓛ 10.00–21.00 Tues–Sat, 10.00–14.00 Sun

Museu d'Art Espanyol Contemporani – Fundació Juan March

A small – but dazzling – display of 20th-century Spanish art, including some priceless treasures by Picasso, Miró and Salvador Dalí, as well as the Mallorcan-born Miquel Barceló. ⓐ C/. de Sant Miquel 11 ⓣ (971) 713515 ⓦ www.march.es/arte/palma ⓛ 10.00–18.30 Mon–Fri, 10.30–14.00 Sat. Admission charge

Museu Diocesà

This quirky museum moved back to its extended and renovated home behind the cathedral in the Episcopal Palace in 2007. It's packed with religious artefacts, historic treasures and holy relics, as well as an impressive collection of ceramics. Highlights include Moorish tapestries, Jaume II's jasper sepulchre and a portrait of St George slaying the dragon, with medieval Palma in the background. ⓐ C/. Mirador 5 ❶ (971) 723860 ⓦ www.bisbatdemallorca.com ⏱ 10.00–14.00 Mon–Sat. Admission charge

Museu de Mallorca

Appropriately enough, Mallorca's leading history museum is contained within a magnificent 17th-century mansion, built on the foundations of one of the island's earliest Arab houses, and located in an atmospheric part of the Old Town. The interior provides a complete overview of Mallorcan history. Temporary exhibitions on local topics add to the museum's appeal. ⓐ C/. Portella 5 ❶ (971) 717540 ⓦ www.museudemallorca.es ⏱ 10.00–19.00 Tues–Sat, 10.00–14.00 Sun. Admission charge

Palau March

A beautiful palace in the city centre, containing a variety of treasures including murals by the great painter Josep Maria Sert, and some fascinating 16th- and 17th-century maps of Mediterranean Europe. The courtyard contains an impressive collection of contemporary sculptures, with works by Rodin, Dalí and Moore. ❸ Palau Reial 18 ❶ (971) 711122 ⓦ www.fundacionmarch.es ⏱ 10.00–18.30 Mon–Fri, 10.00–14.00 Sat, Apr–Oct; 10.00– 17.00 Mon–Fri, 10.00–14.00 Sat, Nov–Mar

RETAIL THERAPY

Start your shopping in the pedestrianised streets leading off Plaça Major – where there are plenty of small, reasonably priced specialist

○ *Palau March – quirky art in a beautiful palace*

shops, interspersed with shoe shops, fashion designers and jewellery boutiques – or explore the trendy boutiques lining Carrer Sant Nicolas and the other narrow streets behind Passeig des Born and Carrer de l'Unio. Also, the best markets are in this part of town: flowers at La Rambla and picnic supplies at Mercat del Olivar.

Adolfo Domínguez One of Spain's most famous designers.
ⓐ C/. Colom 9 ☎ (971) 721565 ⓦ www.adolfo-dominguez.com
🕒 10.00–14.00, 16.30–20.00 Mon–Sat

S'Avarca de Menorca Traditional Menorcan leather sandals.
ⓐ C/. Sant Domingo 14 ☎ (971) 712058 ⓦ www.savarca.com
🕒 10.15–13.30 Mon–Sat (but hours can vary)

Blanc Bleu Stylish, sporty fashions for both sexes. ⓐ C/. Sant Nicolau 22 ⓣ (971) 716983 ⓒ 10.30–14.00, 17.00–20.30 Mon–Sat

Can Frasquet Palma's top chocolate shop. ⓐ C/. Orfila 4 ⓣ (971) 721354 ⓒ 09.30–14.00, 16.45–20.00 Mon–Fri, 10.00–14.00 Sat

Colmado La Montaña A tiny shop with hundreds of sausages hanging from the ceiling; one of the city's top delicatessens. ⓐ C/. de Jaume II 29 ⓣ (971) 712595 ⓒ 10.00–20.00 Mon–Sat

Colmado St Domingo Probably Palma's most photogenic shop, it sells all kinds of tasty local foods. ⓐ C/. Sant Domingo 5 ⓣ (971) 714887 ⓒ 10.00–20.00 Mon–Sat

El Corte Inglés Palma's second branch of this leading, wide-ranging Spanish department store (see page 90). ⓐ Avda. d'Alexandre Rosselló 12 ⓣ (971) 770177 ⓦ www.elcorteingles.es ⓒ 10.00–21.00 Mon–Sat

Custo Another world-famous Catalan designer, this one specialising in patterned t-shirts and retro, A-line coats and skirts. ⓐ C/. Sant Miquel 15 ⓣ (971) 228347 ⓦ www.custo-barcelona.com

Eurocarnavales For a bit of fun, check out this eccentric store, which sells costumes for fiestas. ⓐ C/. de Porta de Jesus 16 ⓣ (971) 722627 ⓒ 09.30–13.45, 17.00–20.30 Mon–Sat

---

◗ *Montaña – definitely the place for sausages*

Fiol Palma's best second-hand bookshop, with excellent English-language stock. 🅰 C/. Oms 45a 🛈 (971) 721428 🕒 10.00–13.30, 17.00–20.00 Mon–Sat

Forn Fondo Shop here for fresh *ensaimadas*. 🅰 C/. de l'Unió 15 🛈 (971) 711634 🕒 08.00–20.30 Mon–Sat, 08.00–14.00 Sun

Imaginarium A magical toy shop, full of sturdy educational toys, games and children's furnishings. 🅰 Pl. Weyler 11 🛈 (971) 714340 🕸 www.imaginarium.es 🕒 10.00–21.00 Mon–Sat

Mercat del Olivar Palma's main market is located in a large hall near Plaça d'Espanya, with fresh produce on the ground floor and meat and cheese upstairs. There are also several cheap tapas stands. 🅰 Pl. Olivar 🛈 (971) 724650 🕒 07.00–14.00 Mon–Sat (open until 20.00 Fri)

La Pajarita A gorgeously traditional shop, split in two; one half functions as a delicatessen, and the other as a patisserie and sweetshop. 🅰 C/. Sant Nicolas 4 🛈 (971) 711844 🕒 09.45–13.45, 17.00–20.00 Mon–Fri, 09.45–13.45 Sat

Pasatiempos The best place in Palma for hunting out cool clubwear. All the hip labels are stocked. 🅰 C/. Quint 3 🛈 (971) 725980 🕸 www.pasatiempos.net 🕒 10.00–20.00 Mon–Sat

Vidrierías Gordiola The best shop in town for glassware. 🅰 C/. de la Victoria 2 🛈 (971) 711541 🕒 10.15–14.00, 16.30–20.00 Mon–Fri, 10.15–14.00 Sat

◑ *It seems a shame to disturb the display by buying something*

TAKING A BREAK

You'll find a large and varied selection of eateries in and around the Old Town. Some are hidden down cool, shady streets in the old Arab quarter, others are clustered around busy squares, and are great for people-watching.

S'Arc £ ❶ A colourful, friendly tapas bar with a good value *menú del día*, just east of the Plaça Major. ❸ Pl. del Banc de l'Oli 13 ❶ (971) 711720 ❿ www.sarctapasyvinos.com ● 09.30–24.00 Mon–Sat

Bar Bosch £ ❷ A café-bar that's long been one of the city's most popular meeting places for a coffee and a light snack. ❸ Pl. Rei Joan Carles I ❶ (971) 721131 ● 07.00–00.30 Mon–Sat, 08.00–01.00 Sun

Bar Cristal £ ❸ One of the oldest cafés in town, with outside tables and a great location. ❸ Pl. Espanya 7 ❶ (971) 721025 ● 07.00–00.30

Blond Café £ ❹ A cool café that's great for coffee and cakes. ❸ Pl. Salvador Coll 10 ❶ (971) 728588 ❿ www.blondcafé.com ● 09.00–23.00 Mon–Sat

Cappuccino Palau March £ ❺ The perfect place to people-watch, or simply to relax on the shaded terrace. ❸ C/. Conquistador 13 ❶ (971) 717272 ❿ www.grupocappuccino.com ● 09.00–24.00 Mon–Fri & Sun, 09.00–02.00 Sat

Ca'n Joan de S'Aigo £ ❻ Pastries, cakes, almond ice cream and scrumptious hot chocolate are all on the menu at this 200-year-old

café in a narrow, winding street. ➋ C/. Ca'n Sanc 10 ➊ (971) 725760
🕐 08.00–21.15 Wed–Fri, 08.00–21.30 Sat & Sun

Fundació La Caixa £ ➐ An elegant bar/restaurant serving excellent
tapas and light dishes. ➋ Pl. Weyler 3 ➊ (971) 728077 🕐 10.00–21.00
Tues–Sat, 10.00–14.00 Sun

Tast £ ➑ A modern informal café-bar, with an open kitchen and
a fab choice of tapas and canapés. ➋ C/. de l'Unio 28 ➊ (971) 729878
🕐 12.30–24.00 Mon–Sat

AFTER DARK

This is not Palma's main party district. Nonetheless, there are still
some excellent restaurants here to suit all tastes and budgets, and
a handful of friendly bars.

RESTAURANTS

Flexas £ ➒ A slightly battered old bar, with changing art
exhibitions on the walls and superb dishes such as baked pork in
red wine and thyme. ➋ C/. Llotgeta 12 ➊ (971) 425938 🕐 10.30–17.00,
20.00–24.00 Mon–Thur, 10.30–17.00, 20.00–01.00 Fri, 12.00–17.00,
20.00–01.00 Sat

Sa Premsa £ ➓ A typical Mallorcan restaurant, with wine vats
around the walls, old bullfighting posters on the walls and cheerful
service. The food is rustic and hearty, with the emphasis on dishes such
as *frito mallorquín* and pork wrapped in cabbage leaves. ➋ Pl. Bisbe
Berenguer de Palou 8 ➊ (971) 723529 🌐 www.cellersapremsa.com
🕐 12.00–16.00, 19.30–23.30 Mon–Sat

◓ *Palma is as cosmopolitan and cultured as other European cities*

La Bodeguilla ££ ⓫ Tradition meets modernity in this intimate tapas bar. Try the *menú degustación* (tasting menu). ⓐ C/. Sant Jaume 3 ⓘ (971) 718274 ⓦ www.la-bodeguilla.com ⓛ 13.00–23.30 Mon–Sat

Es Parlament ££ ⓬ Es Parlament serves light, good-quality Mediterranean fare. ⓐ C/. de Conquistador 11 ⓘ (971) 726026 ⓛ 13.00–15.30, 20.00–22.30 Mon–Sat, closed Sun

Refectori ££ ⓭ Adventurous, globe-trotting cuisine in a calm, minimalist setting inside a converted 17th-century convent. ⓐ C/. de la Missió 7a ⓘ (971) 227347 ⓛ 13.30–15.30, 20.00–22.30 Mon–Fri, 20.00–22.30 Sat

La Taberna del Caracol £££ ⓮ A tavern in one of the oldest buildings in the Old Town, it serves a wide range of outstanding tapas. ⓐ C/. San Alonso 2 ⓘ (971) 714908 ⓛ 13.00–15.15, 19.30–24.00 Mon–Sat May–Sept; 19.30–24.00 Mon–Sat Oct–Apr

CULTURE

Teatre Principal One of Palma's top theatre venues, staging predominantly classical drama, comedies and classical music. ⓐ C/. de la Riera 2 ⓘ (971) 713346 (box office) ⓦ www.teatreprincipalpalma.com.

Ses Voltes A lively open-air venue occupying the filled-in moat between the inner and outer city walls in the Parc de la Mar. It hosts live pop, jazz and rock bands most weekends. ⓐ Parc de la Mar ⓘ (971) 728739 ⓦ www.palmademallorca.es

THE CITY

Western Central Palma

This large area focuses on Palma's magnificent seafront – the Passeig Marítim – which by day is filled with yachtsmen, fishermen, strolling locals and rollerbladers, and after dusk becomes the place to be, with its top-notch restaurants, lively bars and cool clubs. The greatest density of bars and restaurants is in the narrow alleys behind Sa Llotja, but the far end of the Passeig Marítim, around the little harbour of Can Barbará, has its fair share of the action too. Increasingly, one of Palma's hippest places to be is Santa Catalina, a pretty, bohemian neighbourhood to the west of Avinguda Argentina, with no shortage of restaurants and bars.

But this side of town is not just for the party crowd. It also has sights and attractions, including the dazzling new contemporary art gallery, Es Baluard (see page 87), and the historic Castell de Bellver (see page 86) – one of Palma's greatest landmarks.

SIGHTS & ATTRACTIONS

Sa Llotja

This striking building on the seafront was once the maritime exchange, where shipping merchants and commercial traders would do business. Built between 1426 and 1456 by Mallorca's celebrated architect Guillem Sagrera, it has since been used as a granary, and today it is one of the city's most prominent exhibition halls for cultural exhibitions. The exterior is particularly striking – half castle, half church, with turrets and an angel over the doorway – and stands as testament to Palma's former prosperity as a leading maritime centre. Even if you are not interested in the temporary exhibition that is currently on view, it's worth looking inside just to see the

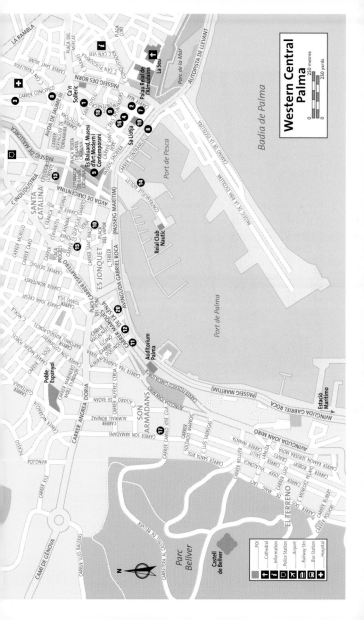

Western Central Palma

0   250 metres
0   250 yards

Badia de Palma

Port de Pesca

Port de Palma

LA RAMBLA

PLAÇA DEL MERCAT

PLAÇA CORT

CARRER SANT JAUME

CAN CAVALLERIA

PLAÇA DE PICCADÒMINE

CARRER SANT FELIU

Ca'n
Solleric

PASSEIG DES BORN

AVDA DE JAUME III

CARRER CONCEPCIÓ

CARRER BERENGUER DE TORNAMIRA

PLAÇA DE LA PORTA SANTA CATALINA

PASSEIG DE MALLORCA

Palau Reial de
l'Almudaina

La Seu

Parc de la Mar

AUTOPISTA DE LLEVANT

CARRER DE LA MAR

CARRER MONTENEGRO

Es Baluard, Museu
d'Art Modern i
Contemporani

Sa Llotja

CARRER SANT JOAN

PASSEIG SAGRERA

CARRER CORDERIA

AVINGUDA DE GABRIEL ROCA

SANTA
CATALINA

C. INDÚSTRIA

CARRER COTONERS

PLAÇA PROGRÉS

CARRER FÀBRICA

CARRER PURSIANA

CARRER ANNIBAL

CARRER SANT MAGÍ

PLAÇA DEL VAPOR

ES JONQUET

AVINGUDA GABRIEL ROCA (PASSEIG MARITIM)

Reial Club
Nàutic

CONTRAMOLLE MOLLET

CARRER CERVANTES

CARRER CARO

CARRER MURILLO

CARRER DESPUIG

CARRER MONTERREY

CARRER SON CORNELLÀ

CARRER ROSSINYOL PORCEL

BARTOMEU ROSSELLÓ PÒRCEL

CARRER MODEL BALAGUER

CARRER TOMÀS VILA

CARRER JOAN CRESPÍ

CARRER MONTERREY

C. MORLÀ

CARRER DEL PONT

CARRER DE LA FINIA

CARRER MAGALHES

CARRER SANTA CREU

Auditòrium
Palma

CARRER BELLVER

CARRER JAUME FERRER

ALMIRALL OQUENDO

AVINGUDA JOAN MIRÓ

CARRER ALFÈREZ CERDÀ

CARRER ÁLVARO DE BAZAN

CARRER SON ARMADANS

CARRER ALMIRALL BONIFAZ

CARRER JOSÉ CELA

CARRER CAMILO JOSÉ CELA

CARRER SOLDADO MAFROIG

CARRER CLUS FÁBREGAS

Poble
Espanyol

CARRER MARINERO MOLL LLIMAGES

CARRER ANDREA DORIA

SON
ARMADANS

EL TERRENO

CARRER BELLVER

CARRER FEDERICO GARCÍA LORCA

AVINGUDA FEDERICO GARCÍA LORCA

PASSEIG MARITIM

Estació
Marítimo

CARRER CASTILLA

CARRER SALUT

CARRER VILLALONGA

CARRER JOSEP

CARRER GRAVES

CARRER SANTA RITA

CARRER DR ROBERT

CARRER RAMÓN FRANCO

AVINGUDA JOAN MIRÓ

CARRER SERVERA MOIA

CARRER INFANTA

CARRER PLANO

CARRER BERBER

CARRER POLXON

CARRER MAC

CARRER DE JOAN

CARRER BLANC

CAMÍ DE GENOVA

CARRER ILLES BALEARS

AVINGUDA JOAN MIRÓ

CARRER ILLE

Parc
Bellver

Castell
de Bellver

CARRETERA AL CASTELL DE BELLVER

N

POI
Cathedral
Information
Police Station
Airport
Railway Stn
Bus Station
Hospital

● *Sa Llotja – once the commercial hub of Palma*

carved pillars and the remarkable rib vaulting in the roof. The area around Sa Llotja is known for its tapas bars and is particularly lively at night. ⓐ Pl. Llotja ❶ (971) 711705 ❸ 11.00–13.45, 17.00–20.45 Tues–Sat, 11.00–13.45 Sun

Passeig des Born
The Passeig des Born has been Palma's main promenade since the early 15th century, when an inlet that once ran here was filled in

after a flood, after which it became a popular venue for fiestas, tournaments and jousting matches. In Franco's day the avenue was renamed Paseo de Generalísimo Franco, but the Mallorquíns refused to use the new name. Today, this grand boulevard is lined with ancient lime trees and flanked by some of the city's smartest shops. Despite the heavy traffic, its central walkway with its flower-filled urns still retains the elegance of bygone days, and its shaded stone benches are a perfect place to rest and watch the world go by.

The Seafront & Port

Palma's magnificent seafront has welcomed visitors to its shores for centuries. The seafront promenade, Passeig Marítim, was built in the 1950s to link the old port of Palma, Porto Pi, with the city centre, and it makes a wonderful walk from Sa Llotja to the passenger ship terminal at the west end of the harbour. Allow about two hours, and then you can catch bus 1 or 50 (from Estació Marítimo 2) back to the city centre.

Start on the pedestrian Passeig Sagrera, with its tall palms and historic maritime buildings, including Sa Llotja and the Renaissance, galleried, Sea Tribunal (Consulat del Mar), impressively decorated with flags and cannons. Cross over to the sea side, and you will pass the small traditional fishing port (Port de Pesca) and the seemingly endless rows of luxury yachts and motorboats flying the flags of many nations. Even though the fishing port is not as active as in the past, you can still see fishermen sitting on the dock mending their nets. It is a particularly magical experience to stroll here at dusk, when the boat lights are sparkling and the cathedral is illuminated.

Continuing along the seafront, look out for the Royal Yacht Club (Reial Club Nautic), patronised by the Spanish royal family and the

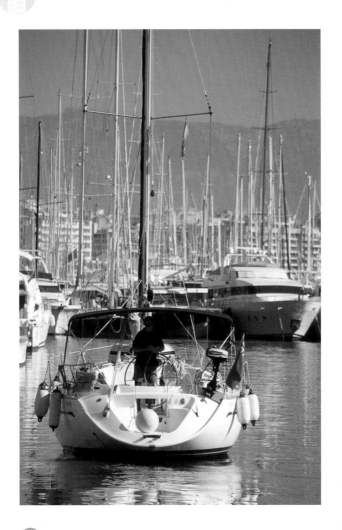

venue of several annual international sailing regattas. To your right you will see five ruined windmills and, in the distance, an excellent view of the Castell de Bellver gracing the skyline. Further on, there is a small monument commemorating the island's celebrated 15th-century cartographers.

Continue past the massive yachts and ostentatious motor cruisers of the Club de Mar until you reach the ship terminal (Estació Marítimo) at the far end, where naval ships, cruise liners and ferries from mainland Spain dock – and you will soon appreciate Palma's long-standing love affair with the sea. There are also plenty of bars, cafés and restaurants for refreshments as you go.

If, however, you prefer to explore Palma's glorious bay by boat, excursion boats offer daytime tours of the harbour from near Sa Llotja (🕐 11.00, 12.00, 13.00, 14.00, 15.00, 16.00 Mon–Sat, 11.00, 12.00, 13.00 Sun) and also a night cruise, from opposite the Auditorium (🕐 22.00 Wed & Sun, June–Sept). There are also day trips to Magaluf, Marineland, Cala Vella, Portals Vells, Sant Elm and Camp de Mar to the west, and to the resorts of Can Pastilla and S'Arenal east of the city. Contact the tourist office for further details.

CULTURE

Palma's arts scene is booming, and nowhere is this more apparent than at Es Baluard (see page 87), the latest addition to an impressive list of modern art museums. On a smaller scale, Ca'n Solleric (see page 88) is just one of several cultural centres which have opened in recent years.

🄌 *Pleasure craft jostle in Palma's busy port*

CASTELL DE BELLVER

This well-preserved circular hill fortress stands sentry above the port, high in the woods about 3 km (2 miles) from the city centre. It was built in the 14th century soon after the Catalan conquest, and is well worth a visit, if only to admire the *bell ver* (beautiful view) of the capital and the bay from its rooftop balcony.

The castle itself – the only circular one in Spain – was built in 1300 as a royal residence during the reign of King Jaume II and is especially unusual in its design. The two-storey structure is built around a central circular courtyard, with three adjoining semi-circular buttressed towers, and a fourth, taller one flanking the castle. The main floor features rounded arches, while the second floor has the pointed arches and ribbed vaulting so typical of Gothic architecture. Over the years the castle has been used as a military prison and as a mint. Today it houses the Palma History Museum and the top floor boasts a striking collection of classical sculptures.

If you're feeling energetic after your visit, make your way back to the city centre on foot. The shaded path starts opposite the entrance to the castle and leads down to Carrer de Bellver and Avinguda de Joan Miró about one km (just over half a mile) below. ⓐ C/. Camilo José Cela 17, Parc Bellver ⓘ (971) 730657 ⓒ 08.00–19.00 Mon–Sat, 10.00–17.00 Sun, Oct–Mar; 08.30–20.30 Mon–Sat, 10.00–19.00, Sun Apr–Sept ⓦ Bus: 50

◆ *The circular layout makes Bellver unique among Spain's castles*

Es Baluard, Museu d'Art Modern i Contemporani

The capital's newest museum – Es Baluard – is a sensational modern and contemporary art museum, built inside the ancient fortress of Sant Pere and Renaissance walls of Palma. The museum has four floors of late 19th- to 21st-century art installations, and two floors are devoted to temporary exhibitions. The ground floor and first floor contain the museum's permanent displays, with emphasis on artworks from the Balearics.

The ground floor contains some fantastic Impressionist and realist paintings of Palma and Mallorcan landscapes. Local and Catalan artists such as Rossello, Ramus, Mir, Rusinyol, Tàpies and Barceló hang alongside works by Cézanne, Matisse, Dalí, Gauguin and Magritte. One section is dedicated to Miró and includes his *Mallorca Series* – nine etchings produced in Palma.

Upstairs, the galleries appear to hang in cleverly suspended spaces above the ground. The highlights here include a room devoted entirely to Picasso ceramics, and the rooftop boardwalk – the Passeig de Ronda – which, punctuated with sculptures, has sweeping views of the city and beyond.

Outside the gallery (at ground level), you can walk on the terraces of the old city walls. These, too, have been converted into a brilliant open-air museum. ❸ Pl. Porta Santa Catalina ❶ (971) 908200 Ⓦ www.esbaluard.org ❶ 10.00–20.00 Tues–Sun, Oct–mid-June, 10.00–22.00 Tues–Sun, mid-June–Sept. Admission charge

Ca'n Solleric

This magnificent Italianate building on the city's main promenade, the Passeig des Born, was constructed for a wealthy family of olive oil merchants in 1763. It was converted in 1995 into a modern art gallery, which hosts a series of temporary exhibitions throughout the year. It now also houses the tourist office, which can provide details of what's currently showing. There is also a small, trendy café-bar adjoining the gallery that makes an ideal light lunch stop for shoppers, and it is also a popular meeting place for early-evening drinks. ❸ Passeig des Born 27 ❶ (971) 722092 Ⓦ www.palmademallorca.es ❶ 10.00–14.00, 17.00–21.00 Tues–Sat, 10.00–13.30 Sun, bar closed Sun evening & Mon

Poble Espanyol

This purpose-built 'Spanish Village' at the heart of a residential district is something of an eccentric attraction. Inside its high walls, you will find faithful reproductions of around 20 important Spanish buildings, including El Greco's house in Toledo and Granada's

◗ *Es Baluard – modern art in an ancient setting*

Alhambra palace. These are then surrounded by typical houses from various Spanish regions, providing visitors with a whistle-stop tour of Spanish architecture. In the buildings are various craft studios that demonstrate a variety of local skills, a café and a host of souvenir shops selling everything from Mallorcan pearls to castanets. ➌ C/. Poble Espanyol 39 ➊ (971) 737075 ➍ www.congress-palace-palma.com ◷ 09.00–19.00 Apr–Sept, 09.00–18.00 Oct–Mar (shops close Sat afternoon and Sun). Admission charge

RETAIL THERAPY

This is the district for serious shoppers, as it embraces Avinguda Jaume III, an elegant, arcaded avenue containing Palma's most sophisticated shops. Here too is the high-quality department store El Corte Inglés (see below), and in Passeig des Born is a variety of popular chain stores, chic boutiques and specialist shops.

Es Baluard The museum shop of Palma's modern art gallery sells an impressive range of arty gifts, calendars, ceramics, mobiles, silk scarves and beautiful coffee-table books. ➌ Pl. Porta Santa Catalina ➊ (971) 908200 ➍ www.esbaluard.org ◷ 10.00–20.00 Tues–Sun, Oct–mid-June; 10.00–23.00 Tues–Sun, mid-June–Sept

El Corte Inglés One of two branches of Spain's leading department stores in Palma, selling everything from designer fashions to electronics, books, toys, jewellery and cosmetics. There is also a full supermarket, cafeteria and restaurant, and the Gourmet Club delicatessen on the second floor offers over 1,000 varieties of wine, oils, cheeses

◗ *A walk around Poble Espanyol is a holiday in itself*

and other gastronomic delights. ⓐ Avda. Jaume III 15 ☏ (971) 770177
Ⓦ www.elcorteingles.es ⏰ 10.00–21.30 Mon–Sat

Loewe One of the most celebrated leather-goods companies in
the world. ⓐ Avda. Jaume III 1 ☏ (971) 715275 Ⓦ www.loewe.es
⏰ 10.00–20.00 Mon–Sat

Majorica The main city branch of Mallorca's leading pearl
manufacturer. ⓐ Avda. Jaume III 11 ☏ (971) 725268 Ⓦ www.majorica.es
⏰ 09.30–13.30 Mon–Sat, 16.30–20.00 Mon–Fri

Mango A nationwide chain of trendy fashion stores, popular with
young fashionistas on a budget. ⓐ Avda. Jaume III 9 ☏ (971) 713896
Ⓦ www.mango.com ⏰ 10.00–21.00 Mon–Sat

Persépolis Palma's premier antiques shop is a fascinating place
to browse. ⓐ Avda. Jaume III 23 ☏ (971) 724539 ⏰ 09.30–13.30,
16.30–20.00 Mon–Fri, 09.30–13.00 Sat

Relojería Alemana This upmarket shop sells all the top names in
designer watches and jewellery, as well as fine silver tableware and
Mallorcan grandfather clocks. ⓐ Avda. Jaume III 26 ☏ (971) 716712
⏰ 09.30–13.30, 16.30–20.00 Mon–Fri, 09.30–13.30 Sat

TAKING A BREAK

You'll be spoilt for choice of eateries in the Sa Llotja district of
town, with its countless restaurants and tapas bars in the maze
of narrow streets and alleys just off Passeig des Born and Avinguda
Antoni Maura.

Bon Lloc £ ❶ One of Palma's few vegetarian restaurants, with a good-value four-course set lunch. Ⓐ C/. Sant Feliu 7 ❶ (971) 718617 🕐 13.00–16.00 Mon–Sat

La Boveda £ ❷ Definitely the best tapas bar in Palma. Ⓐ C/. Boteria 3 (off Carrer Mar) ❶ (971) 714863 🕐 13.30–16.00, 20.30–23.45 Mon–Fri, 13.30–16.00, 20.30–00.30 Sat

El Burladero £ ❸ Among the huge variety of tapas, the *cazuelitas* (tiny casserole dishes) of stews stand out. Ⓐ C/. Concepció 36 ❶ (971) 713459 Ⓦ www.burladero-restaurantes.com 🕐 10.30–16.30, 19.00–01.00 Mon–Sat

Café La Lonja £ ❹ A handsome bar in a *belle époque* style, with lots of carved wood fittings. Tapas are served, along with excellent wines. Ⓐ C/. Llotja del Mar 2 (off C/. dels Apuntadors) ❶ (971) 722799 🕐 09.30–01.00 Mon–Thur, 09.30–03.00 Fri & Sat

Museu Es Baluard £ ❺ Modern Mallorquín al fresco dining on a shaded terrace or in the cool, white minimalist dining room overlooking the port. Excellent salads, soups and seafood. Ⓐ Pl. Porta Santa Catalina s/n ❶ (971) 908200 🕐 13.00–16.00, 20.00–23.00 Tues–Sun

Port Pesquer £ ❻ This chic waterfront café serves delicious fresh fish and tapas from midday to midnight. Ⓐ Passeig Marítim s/n, opposite Sa Llotja ❶ (971) 715220 🕐 10.00–01.00 (until 03.00 Thur–Sat)

Xim's Bodeguita £ ❼ One of several hugely popular pavement cafés serving tapas in Plaça Llotja. Ⓐ Pl. de Sa Llotja 3 (off Carrer Mar) ❶ (971) 719928 🕐 11.00–22.00

AFTER DARK

If you're looking for the trendiest hangouts, this is the district for you. Sa Llotja boasts the highest density of restaurants and bars (with Santa Catalina hot on its tail), but for night owls the Passeig Marítim is the place to be, with its countless late-bars and nightclubs all revelling to the Balearic beat. Also check out the laid-back bars around the small inlet of Can Barbará.

RESTAURANTS

Can Carlos £ ❽ Tucked down a back-street just off the fashionable Avinguda Jaume III, this traditional-style restaurant specialises in authentic *cuina mallorquina*. Try their tasty *tumbet* or the hearty *frito mallorquín*. ❸ C/. de S'Aigua 5 (off Avda de Jaume III) ❶ (971) 713869 ❺ 13.15–16.00 Mon–Sat, 20.00–23.15 Thur–Sat

La Cueva £ ❾ A small but lively tapas restaurant, where hams hang from the ceiling. ❸ C/. dels Apuntadors 5 ❶ (971) 724422 ❺ 12.30–13.30 Mon–Sat

Diner £ ❿ An all-American, 24-hour burger bar, complete with shakes, fries, apple pie and a jukebox. ❸ C/. Sant Magí 23 ❶ (971) 736222

Arroceríes Sa Cranca ££ ⓫ The speciality of this restaurant on the seafront is paella, freshly cooked to order and served in a number of different styles, including vegetarian. ❸ Passeig Marítim 13 ❶ (971) 737447 ❺ 13.00–15.30, 20.00–23.30 Tues–Sat. 13.00–15.30 Sun

Baisakhi ££ 🄬 A highly rated Indian restaurant on the seafront.
🄰 Passeig Marítim 8 🄣 (971) 736806 🄛 20.00–24.00 Tues–Sun

Le Bistrot ££ 🄭 Stylish French cuisine in a Parisian-style bistro.
🄰 C/. Teodoro Llorente 4 🄣 (971) 287175 🄛 13.00–16.00,
20.30–24.00 Mon–Sat

Ca'n Eduardo ££ 🄮 One of the city's premier fish restaurants,
located in the fishing port. 🄰 C/. Industria Pesquera 4 🄣 (971) 721182
🄛 13.00–15.30, 20.00–23.00 Mon–Sat

Fábrica 23 ££ 🄯 Fábrica 23 offers a menu of stellar dishes –
some Mallorcan and some from elsewhere in the Mediterranean.
🄰 C/. Cotoner 42 🄣 (971) 453125 🄦 www.fabrica23.com
🄛 13.00–15.30, 21.00–23.30 Tues–Sat

Orient Express ££ 🄰 Top-notch *crêpes* and tapas served in
a carriage of the great Orient Express. 🄰 C/. Llotja del Mar 6
(off C/. dels Apuntadors) 🄣 (971) 711183 🄛 13.30–16.00, 20.30–24.00
Mon–Fri, 08.30–24.00 Sat

Shogun ££ 🄱 Palma's most popular Japanese restaurant.
🄰 C/. Camilo José Cela 14 🄣 (971) 735748 🄛 13.00–15.30,
20.00–23.30 🄝 Bus: 3, 6, 50

Aramis £££ 🄲 One of the best restaurants in Palma, with a simple,
smart interior and modern Mediterranean cuisine. 🄰 C/. Montenegro 1
🄣 (971) 725232 🄦 www.restaurante-aramis.com 🄛 13.00–17.00 Mon–Fri,
20.00–24.00 Mon–Sat

Caballito de Mar £££ ⑲ Fresh fish and seafood dishes, such as sea bass baked in rock salt, are the specialities at this busy seafront restaurant. ⓐ Passeig Sagrera 5 ⓣ (971) 721074 ⓦ www.caballito demar.info ⓛ 13.00– 16.00, 19.30–23.30 Tues–Thur, 13.00–16.00, 20.00–24.00 Fri & Sat

Koldo Royo £££ ⑳ Basque chef Koldo Royo's imaginative Mediterranean nouvelle cuisine and comprehensive wine list have made his eponymous restaurant on the sea promenade one of the island's finest. ⓐ Passeig Marítim 3 ⓣ (971) 732435 ⓦ www.koldoroyo.com. ⓛ 13.00–16.00 Tues–Fri, 20.30–24.00 Mon–Sat

CULTURE
Auditorium Palma's premier showbiz venue, located on the waterfront and staging theatre, opera, classical concerts and ballet. ⓐ Passeig Marítim ⓣ (971) 735 328 (information), (971) 734735 (tickets) ⓦ www.auditoriumpalma.com.

Teatre Municipal This theatre frequently features contemporary drama, classic films, dance and ballet. ⓐ Passeig Mallorca 9b ⓣ (971) 739148/ 710986 (box office)

BARS & NIGHTCLUBS
Abaco Palma's most unusual cocktail bar is situated inside a 17th-century palace, with caged birds, fountains, candles, classical music and huge baskets of fruit. ⓐ C/. Sant Joan 1 ⓣ (971) 714939 ⓛ 20.00– 01.00 Sun–Thur, 20.00–03.00 Fri & Sat

Abraxas This popular nightclub attracts a young crowd. ⓐ Passeig Marítim 42 ⓣ (971) 455908 ⓦ www.abraxasmallorca.com ⓛ 23.00–06.00

Barbero A small disco bar playing everything including house, jazz, funk, blues and soul. Don't try to call to see who's on: they don't have a phone. ⓐ C/. Jaume Ferrer 3 🕒 23.00–03.00 Wed–Sat

La Bodeguita del Medio Cuban rhythms, wicked daiquiris and rum-drenched *mojitos*. Well lively. ⓐ C/. de Vallseca 18 ☎ (971) 717832 ⓦ www.labodeguitadelmedio.com 🕒 22.00–03.30 Wed–Sun

Garito's This groovy, split-level bar attracts a young, pre-clubbing crowd and, at weekends, plays host to the hippest DJs in town. ⓐ Darsena de Can Barbarà ☎ (971) 736912 ⓦ www.garitocafe.com 🕒 18.00–04.00

Harbour Club By day, local yachties congregate at the cool white and turquoise poolside bar of the city's newest chill-out zone in the Club de Mar yacht club. By night, its chic terrace, lounges and bars are the latest favourite haunt of the beautiful people of Palma. ⓐ Club de Mar, Moll Pelaires ☎ (971) 289946 ⓦ www.harbourclubpalma.com 🕒 09.00–24.00

Soho Urban Vintage Bar A gloriously retro bar, decorated with 70s wallpaper and battered album covers. ⓐ Avda. Argentina 5 ☎ (971) 454719 🕒 09.00–02.00 Mon–Thur, 09.00–03.30 Fri & Sat

Tito's Palma's largest, most famous and rather commercial nightclub. ⓐ Passeig Marítim, s/n ☎ (971) 730017 ⓦ www.titosmallorca.com 🕒 23.00–06.00 Thur–Sun

The Bay of Palma

The Badia de Palma (Bay of Palma) has some of Spain's finest beaches, with limpid turquoise waters, though their popularity doesn't always make for an especially tranquil experience. The beaches to the west of Palma cater mostly to a British crowd, while to the east of the city you'll hear more German than any other language, including Spanish. Children, however, will be in heaven, not only with the beaches, but with the caves, the waterparks and the magic of the sea, and the adults can relax, knowing that the kids are having fun. Those who like nothing better than soaking up the sun, will definitely be spoilt for choice, while night owls will thrive in some of the wildest party resorts.

Once you get beyond Portal Nous to the West and Ciutat Jardí to the East, the deeper you get into bucket-and-spade country, with fewer cultural sights and an increasing number of theme parks and family attractions. The resorts are easy to reach by local bus. They vary hugely in character, from glitzy Porto Portals and the hip new suburb of Es Molinar to Magaluf, Mallorca's legendary nightlife capital.

SIGHTS & ATTRACTIONS

The various beaches and resorts of the Bay of Palma are fantastic places to take all the family to escape the bustle of the city and to soak up the sun and relax, perhaps with a picnic. Allow a whole day for the theme parks, and also for Festival Park (see page 103) if you are a keen shopaholic.

S'Arenal
The bustling resort of S'Arenal sits at one end of the long Platja de Palma, more than 5 km (3 miles) of wide, sandy beach, with the twin

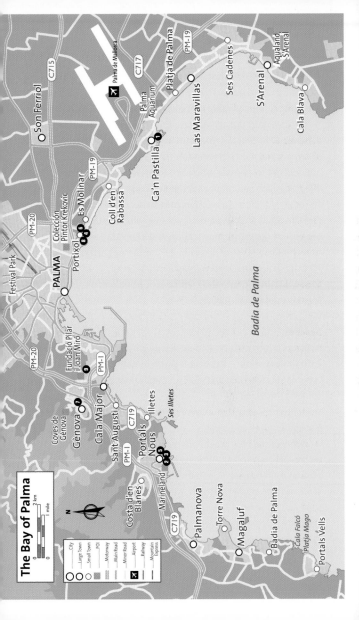

The Bay of Palma

0   1 km
0   1 mile

N

City
Large Town
Small Town
POI
Motorway
Main Road
Minor Road
Airport
Railway
Mountain
Express

Son Ferriol

C715

Festival Park

PM-20

PALMA

Colección Pintor Krekovic

Portixol

Es Molinar

Coll d'en Rabassa

Palma Aquarium

Ca'n Pastilla

Platja de Palma

Las Maravillas

Ses Cadenes

S'Arenal

Aqualand S'Arenal

Cala Blava

PM-19

C717

Palma de Mallorca

Fundació Pilar i Joan Miró

PM-1

PM-20

Coves de Génova

Génova

Cala Major

Sant Augustí

Illetes

Ses Illetes

Portals Nous

Costa d'en Blanes

Marineland

C719

Palmanova

Torre Nova

Magaluf

Badia de Palma

Cala Falcó
Platja Mago

Portals Vells

Badia de Palma

resort of Ca'n Pastilla at the other end. The resorts have a highly international flavour, with English pubs, German and Dutch bars, and visitors from all over Europe converging on the beach.

A particularly popular and exciting draw here is **Aqualand S'Arenal** (🄰 Palma – S'Arenal motorway, exit 13 🛈 (971) 440000 🄦 www.aqualand.es/elarenal/mallorca), which has enough thrills and spills to keep kids amused and entertained all day. Older children will enjoy such hair-raising rides as Kamikaze and Black Hole, though fortunately there are also other, more sedate, rides for younger children (and cautious parents). Among the many other attractions are go-karting, parrot shows, falconry demonstrations and a mini-farm. Aqualand has, incidentally, a sister theme park in Magaluf (🄦 www. www.aqualand.es/magaluf/mallorca).

S'Arenal Tourist Information Office 🄰 Pl. Reina Maria Cristina, s/n 🛈 (971) 440414 🄝 Bus: 15, 23

Beaches

Mallorca prides itself on its beaches, which are generally very clean, with shallow water – bathwater-warm during the summer, making them safe for children and ideal for family holidays. Palma Bay boasts some of the island's finest beaches – from magnificent, long, sandy stretches packed with holidaymakers to tiny deserted coves with transparent turquoise water.

Some of the best beaches in the bay include those at the resorts of Magaluf and Palmanova and the 7 km (4 mile) stretch of sand running from Can Pastilla to S'Arenal, all of which in recent years have been given facelifts, with new promenades, imported sand and improved watersports facilities. There are also pleasant,

---

● *There's a wide choice of sandy beaches near Palma*

albeit smaller, beaches at Cala Major, Illetes and Portals Nous. Alternatively, seek out one of the deserted inlets and pine-shaded *calas* (coves) indenting the wild rocky coastline south of Magaluf, including Cala Falcó, Platja Mago (popular for nude sunbathing) and Cala Portals Vells.

Ca'n Pastilla & Platja de Palma

Just five minutes from Palma Town, these two resorts merge smoothly into one another as you stroll along the main promenade. Ideal for families, young and old, days are spent lazing on the broad sandy beach which stretches for 7 km (4 miles) as far as S'Arenal, or enjoying the various watersports on offer, including water-skiing, windsurfing and pedalo hire. At night, choose between living it up in one of the many bars and discos or enjoying a quiet meal on the seafront overlooking the beautiful bay of Palma from an array of international restaurants.

Platja de Palma Tourist Information Office ⓐ Pl. Meravelles, s/sn ❶ (971) 264532 ⓝ Bus: 15, 17, 23

Coves de Gènova (Caves of Gènova)

These spectacular underground caverns, with their chambers of vividly illuminated stalactites and stalagmites, can be found in the characterful village of Gènova, high on the slopes of the Serra de Na Burguesa hills above Palma. Gènova itself has a surprisingly high number of traditional-style restaurants for its size, and is especially popular with Mallorcan families.

ⓐ C/. de Barranc, Gènova ❶ (971) 402387 ❶ 10.00–13.30, 16.00–19.00, Apr–Oct; 10.00–13.00, 16.00–18.00, Nov–Mar ⓝ Bus: 4. Admission charge

Festival Park

Just 15 minutes from Palma, this spacious leisure complex provides a good day out for all the family with its enormous range of facilities and activities, including 26 different shops and factory outlets, 30 restaurants, two cinemas, 22-lane bowling, not to mention the largest reptilarium in Europe and the Mallorca Rural Museum, containing over 500 miniature model scenes of rural life and trades of the past on the island. There's even open-air evening entertainment in the centre square. ⓐ Autopista Palma-Inca, Km 7, 1 ⓣ (971) 226822 ⓦ www.festivalpark.es ⓛ times vary, check website for details ⓝ Bus: 20

Illetes

A quiet, low-key resort, with two good beaches overlooking Palma Bay, this is a popular weekend outing destination for families from Palma – with the result that it is by far the most Spanish of the Bay of Palma resorts. ⓐ Carretera Andratx 33 ⓝ Bus: 3

Magaluf

Magaluf, more than anywhere else, exemplifies the rapid growth of Mallorcan tourism. What was once no more than a quiet fishing village on the western edge of Palma Bay has been transformed into a pulsating mega-resort, where the summer months have become one long, continuous party.

The beach, with its long seafront promenade, is one of the best on the island, and if you fancy something more energetic than sunbathing there are canoes and pedalos for hire – as well as windsurfing and snorkelling equipment, boat trips and even a two-hour underwater excursion in a Nemo Submarine. Children will love Aqualand (see page 100) and **Karting Magaluf** ((971) 131734 www.kartingmagaluf.com). But most visitors to Magaluf save their energy for the nightlife. From discos and cocktail bars to rip-roaring dinner shows and dubious 'adult entertainment', Mallorca's nocturnal capital has it all.

Magaluf Tourist Information Office C/. Pere Vaquer Ramis 1 (971) 131126 www.visitcalvia.com Bus: 103, 104, 105, 106, 107

Marineland

Performing dolphins, sea lions and parrots are the star turns at this sea-life centre, and there is also a penguin pool, a reptile house and an aquarium with sharks and tropical fish on display. Children have fun on the miniature train or playing in the adventure playground and the mock pirate ship. C/. Garcilaso de la Vega 9, Costa d'En Blanes (971) 675125 www.marineland.es 09.30–17.00 Jan–Nov (18.00 July & Aug) Bus: 103, 104, 106, 107, 111

Palma Aquarium

Palma's newest attraction, situated out near the airport, is this vast aquarium, housing over 8,000 specimens of marine life. There are 55 different aquariums displaying a variety of habitats, but the most popular, naturally, is the shark tank. A glass tunnel running through the middle allows visitors to get terrifyingly close. C/. Manuela de los Herreros i Soria 21 (971) 264275 www.palmaaquarium.com 10.00–18.00. Admission charge

Palmanova

'New Palma' is beautifully situated on a wide, sandy bay to the west of Palma. Sandwiched between the ritzy harbour at Porto Portals and the riotous nightlife of Magaluf, it's an excellent resort

for families, with golden beaches and a wide choice of restaurants.
Children especially enjoy the watersports and Golf Fantasia,
one of the best mini-golf courses on the island.

Palmanova Tourist Information Office ⓐ Passeig de la Mar 13
ⓘ (971) 682365 Ⓝ Bus: 103, 104, 105, 106, 107

Porto Portals – Portals Nous

Portals Nous is the St Tropez of the Balearics. Its glitzy harbour – Porto
Portals – is considered to be the best yachting marina in the area.
Crammed with de luxe boutiques and fashionable restaurants and

⬢ *Portals Nous is the Balearics' most upmarket resort*

bars, it is a great venue for people-watching and celebrity-spotting.

ⓐ Portals Nous ⓝ Bus: 103, 104, 106, 107, 111

Portixol/Es Molinar

The suburb of Es Molinar and the small bay of Portixol, with its own harbour, marina and tiny beach, are within easy walking distance to the east of Palma. In the last five years this sleepy fishing district has flourished and it now boasts a beautiful promenade, a chic boutique hotel and some of the hippest restaurants in Mallorca.

ⓝ Bus: 15, 17, 18

CULTURE

While there is much to see on the fringes of the city, the plentiful art and culture of the centre begins to dry up the further afield you go in the Bay of Palma. However, the Colección Pintor Krekovic (see below), in the eastern outskirts, is worth a visit, and the magnificent Fundació Pilar i Joan Miró (see opposite), in Cala Major to the west, counts among the island's most important galleries.

Colección Pintor Krekovic

This small museum in Querétaro, an eastern suburb of Palma, is devoted to the romantic paintings of the Croatian artist Kristian Krekovic, who lived in Palma for the last 20 years of his life until his death in 1985. His bold-coloured paintings cover themes as diverse as the early civilisations of South America, Spanish daily life and his homeland. ⓐ C/. Ciutat de Querétaro 3 ⓣ (971) 219606 ⓛ 09.30–13.00, 15.00–18.00 Mon–Fri, 09.30–13.00 Sat, closed Aug ⓝ Bus: 12, 18. Admission charge

A ROYAL ISLAND

The Spanish royal family holidays in Mallorca at least three times a year, in the aptly named Palau Marivent ('*Mar i Vent*' means 'Wind and Sea') – an impressive waterfront villa in Cala Major. Their visits usually coincide with major sporting events, including the Princess Sofia Cup sailing regatta at Easter and the HRH Princess Elena Showjumping Cup in August.

Fundació Pilar i Joan Miró (Pilar and Joan Miró Gallery), Cala Major

The abstract Catalan artist Joan Miró lived on Mallorca for much of his life, and his house and studio have been turned into a museum of his work, with a fantastically modern and spacious interior, using water, concrete and light to juxtapose his splashy canvases of primary colours. The garden contains several sculptures and a café, while his studio (which opens at 11.00) has been left largely untouched since his death in 1983, with tins of paint still lying around open on the tables. The museum is in the heart of the lively, popular suburb of Cala Major, with its magnificent sandy beach, good restaurants, shops and bars. Apart from the museum, the resort's most prestigious address is Palau Marivent (see above), a villa owned by the King of Spain. ⓐ C/. Joan de Saridakis 29, Cala Major ⓣ (971) 701420 ⓦ miro.palmademallorca.es ⓛ 10.00–18.00 (19.00 during summer months) Tues–Sat, 10.00–15.00 Sun ⓝ Bus: 3, 6

RETAIL THERAPY

Carrefour If you are staying in self-catering accommodation, this huge hypermarket on the northern outskirts of Palma provides

quick and easy one-stop shopping for your holiday. ⓐ Avda.
General Riera 152 (clearly signposted from the Via Cintura ring
road) ⓣ (971) 766300 ⓦ www.carrefour.es ⓛ 09.30–21.30 Mon–Sat
ⓝ Bus: 16

Festival Park Pick up some bargains from the likes of Levis, Reebok,
Quiksilver, Nike and Mango at this huge factory outlet centre, and
visit the summer crafts market (18.00–23.00 Fri–Sat) for some
local souvenirs and handicrafts. ⓐ Autopista Palma-Inca, Km 7.1
ⓣ (971) 226822 ⓦ www.festivalpark.es ⓛ 10.00–22.00 Mon–Sat,
11.00–22.00 Sun ⓝ Bus: 20

Fundacio Pilar i Joan Miró A tiny gift shop in the basement of the
Joan Miró museum that has a wonderful range of unusual gifts,
including arty Miró mugs and t-shirts, jewellery, books and *siurells* –
clay whistles resembling a man in a hat playing a guitar or sitting
on a donkey, painted white with flashes of red and green – which
have been made in Mallorca and given as tokens of friendship since
Arab times. Miró was said to have been much influenced by their
brightness and simplicity. ⓐ C/. Joan de Saridakis 29, Cala Major
ⓣ (971) 701420 ⓛ 10.00–18.00 (19.00 during summer months)
Tues–Sat, 10.00–15.00 Sun ⓝ Bus: 3, 6

Porto Pi The massive Porto Pi hypermarket-cum-shopping centre at
the western end of the Passeig Marítim has over 100 shops under
one roof, including a Carrefour hypermarket, fashion boutiques,
delicatessens, eateries and ice-cream parlours, gifts and handicraft
shops, and a safe play area for children. ⓐ Avda. Gabriel Roca 54
ⓣ (971) 701530 ⓛ 10.00–22.00 Mon–Sat ⓝ Bus: 1, 14, 50

TAKING A BREAK

Many of the bars and restaurants in the After Dark section
(see page 110) also serve food and drinks during the day.

Anima Sea Lounge £ ❶ A fusion restaurant with a sunny terrace
overlooking the beach. ⓐ C/. Pins 17, Cala Estància ☎ (971) 745437
ⓦ www.animasealounge.com 🕒 12.00–02.00 Tues–Sun (winter);
12.00–23.00 (summer)

Diablito £ ❷ A popular waterfront pizzeria overlooking the boats
in the Porto Portals marina. ⓐ Porto Portals Locale 41 ☎ (971) 676503
ⓦ www.diablitofoodandmusic.com 🕒 09.00–24.00 🚌 Bus: 103, 104,
106, 107, 111

Flanigan £ ❸ A Porto Portals institution that serves a hearty
breakfast and the house speciality – apple tart. ⓐ Porto Portals
Locale 17, Portals Nous ☎ (971) 679191 🕒 13.00–23.00 🚌 Bus: 103,
104, 106, 107, 111

Minimar £ ❹ Trendy tapas bar in a prime location on the seafront
at Portixol. Fish and shellfish predominate. ⓐ C/. Vicari Joaquin
Fuster 67, Portixol ☎ (971) 248604 ⓦ www.grupocappuccino.com
🕒 Restaurant 13.00–16.00, 19.30–23.00; Bar 13.00–23.00
🚌 Bus: 15, 17, 18

Tahini £ ❺ Taste the freshest of fish at this sophisticated sushi bar.
ⓐ Porto Portals Locale 2 ☎ (971) 676025 ⓦ www.grupocappuccino.com
🕒 13.00–15.30, 19.30–23.00 🚌 Bus: 103, 104, 106, 107, 111

AFTER DARK

From traditional Mallorquín cuisine in old-fashioned country restaurants to fine fish in trendy minimalist seafront cafés, the Bay of Palma has it all. It also enjoys some of the finest nightlife on the island, embracing the newly fashionable suburb of Portixol/Es Molinar, the upmarket night haunts of Porto Portals, two major new beach party venues, lively theme evenings, and the tourist-touting mega-disco BCM (see page opposite) in the notorious resort of Magaluf.

RESTAURANTS

Bar, Co £ ❻ Some of the best food in Palma is to be had in this unassuming little restaurant. Inventive Asian dishes incorporate elements from all around the globe. ⓐ C/. Vicari Joaquim Fuster 83 ❶ (971) 248685 ❺ 13.00–24.00 Wed–Sun

Ca'n Pedro £ ❼ Snails are a speciality at this traditional-style restaurant. ⓐ C/. de Rector Vives 14, Gènova ❶ (971) 402479 ❺ 12.30–16.30, 19.00–00.30 Thur–Tues ❽ Bus: 4

Rocamar ££ ❽ A top-notch fish and seafood restaurant, with black minimalist décor and a stylish terrace, frequented by Palma's smart set. ⓐ C/. Vicario Joaquin Fuster 1, Portixol ❶ (971) 274644 ❺ 13.30–23.30 Tues–Sun ❽ Bus: 15, 17, 18

Samantha's £££ ❾ Dine in style in a traditional villa in Bonanova, overlooking the Bay of Palma and Bellver Castle. The Mediterranean cuisine is sensational and there is also an impressive wine list. ⓐ C/. Francesc Vidal i Sureda 115

☏ (971) 700000 🌐 www.restaurantesamanthas.com
🕐 13.00–16.00, 20.00–23.00 🚌 Bus: 6

BARS & NIGHTCLUBS

Abacanto A sophisticated cocktail bar in a lavish mansion in the suburb of Indioteria. 📍 Camino de Son Nicolau, s/n, Indoteria ☏ (971) 430624 🌐 www.abacanto.es 🕐 20.00–01.30 Mon–Thurs & Sun, 21.00–02.30 Fri & Sat, closed Nov–Mar 🚌 Bus: 10

BCM One of Europe's largest discos, with spectacular laser shows, swimming pool, foam parties and big-name DJs. 📍 Avda. S'Olivera, s/n, Magaluf ☏ (971) 132609 🌐 www.bcm-planetdance.com 🕐 20.00–04.30 🚌 Bus: 103, 104, 105, 106, 107

Kaskai An ultra-cool bar on the seafront at Es Molinar, with tables spilling out onto the pavement. The perfect setting for *una copa romantica*. 📍 C/. Vicario Joaquin Fuster 71, Portixol ☏ (971) 241284 🕐 24.00–02.30 Thur–Tues 🚌 Bus: 17, 18

Puro Beach One of the the latest additions to the party scene, this new beach- and poolside bar venue near the airport draws the beautiful people of Palma by day for yoga, cocktails and chilling out, but by night it comes alive for vibrant sunset parties. 📍 C/. Pagell 12 ☏ (971) 744744 🕐 24.00–02.30 Thur–Tues 🌐 www.purobeach.com

Virtual Club A sophisticated beach club by day that dissolves into a beach party at sundown, with a spectacular bar set in natural caves. 📍 Passeig d'Illetes 60 ☏ (971) 703235 🌐 www.virtualclub.es 🕐 10.00–24.00 Fri & Sat 🚌 Bus: 3

CINEMA & ENTERTAINMENT

Ocimax A leisure centre on the outskirts of Palma that has 15 cinema screens (with a few films in English), 26-lane bowling and a wide choice of restaurants and bars. ⓐ Carretera Valldemossa, s/n ⓣ (971) 750673 ⓦ www.ocimax.com ⓝ Bus: 12

Pirate's Adventure A great family night out, with a swashbuckling pirates adventure show. Booking is advised. ⓐ Carretera de sa Porrassa ⓣ (971) 130411 ⓦ www.piratesadventure.com ⓛ family show at 18.00 and 20.00; adult show at 21.00 and 23.00 ⓝ Bus: 103, 104, 105, 106, 107

Son Amar A fun, spectacular, all-singing and all-dancing late-night show, in a converted 16th-century mansion that's a ten-minute drive north of Palma. ⓐ Carretera de Soller, Km 10, Bunyola ⓛ 19.30–00.01 ⓣ (971) 617533/ (900) 712345 ⓦ www.sonamar.com

ⓞ *Fornalutx is regarded as one of Spain's prettiest villages*

OUT OF TOWN
trips

Valldemossa & Deià

The northwestern coastline contains some of the most spectacular scenery on Mallorca, with pine-scented forests and terraced hillsides tumbling into the sea. This corner of Mallorca has long appealed to foreigners – Frédéric Chopin and Robert Graves were both drawn here, and Michael Douglas and Andrew Lloyd Webber own homes in the area. Hire a car (or ask your holiday rep about daytrips) to visit the 'celebrity' mountain villages of Deià and Valldemossa and the surrounding countryside, to see the best that the region has to offer.

GETTING THERE

During the week there are eight buses to Valldemossa and four that continue to Deià from Palma. On Saturday there are two buses to each destination, while on Sunday there are six to Valldemossa and two to Deià. By car Valldemossa is 23 km (14 miles) from Palma on the MA 1130, and Deià is another 16 km (10 miles) further along.

VALLDEMOSSA

Valldemossa is one of the best-known villages in Mallorca, and is located just 15 km (10 miles) north of Palma in the Tramuntana Mountains. Here Frédéric Chopin and his mistress, the French authoress George Sand, spent the winter of 1838 here. The scenery has changed little since, and Valldemossa remains well worth visiting.

Valldemossa is also the birthplace of the island's patron saint, Santa Catalina Tomás, and nearly every house in the village has a painted tile beside the front door asking for the saint's protection. Today, it is better known as the second home of Hollywood royalty

◔ *Hiking along a bridle path in the Serra de Tramuntana near Valldemossa*

Michael Douglas and Catherine Zeta-Jones. Douglas has owned
a country estate here for over 20 years. He sponsored a cultural
centre in the village, Costa Nord, which hosts frequent concerts
and during the day shows a documentary recounting the history
of this region, narrated by Douglas himself.

SIGHTS & ATTRACTIONS
Port de Valldemossa
If you are brave enough to negotiate the 6 km (4 mile) helter-skelter
drive that separates Valldemossa from its coastal port, you will enjoy
numerous dramatic viewpoints and hair-raising hairpin bends before
entering the charming fishing village of Port de Valldemossa. Here
you will discover a handful of stone cottages, fishing boats and
a small stony beach – perfect for a light lunch before setting off
again up the corkscrew road.

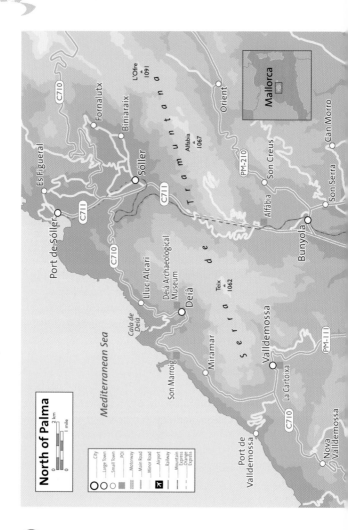

North of Palma

Mallorca

Mediterranean Sea

C710
Es Figueral
Fornalutx
L'Ofre ▲ 1091
Biniaraix
Sóller
C711
Orient
Can Morro
Alfàbia ▲ 1067
Tramuntana
de
Serra
PM-210
Son Creus
Son Serra
Port de Sóller
C711
C711
Alfàbia
C710
Bunyola
Lluc-Alcari
Deià Archaeological Museum
Deià
Teix ▲ 1062
Cala de Deià
Miramar
Valldemossa
Son Marroig
La Cartoixa
PM-111
Port de Valldemossa
C710
Nova Valldemossa

0 — 2 km
0 — 1 mile

City
Large Town
Small Town
POI
Motorway
Main Road
Minor Road
Airport
Railway
Mountain
Express
Orange
Express

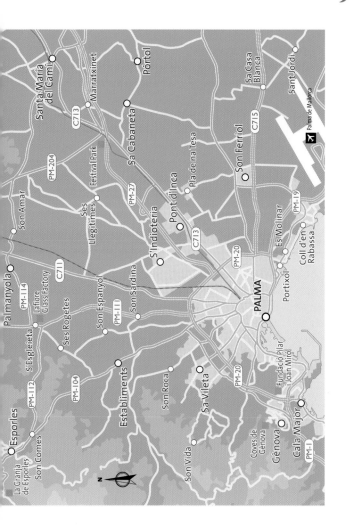

Santa Maria del Camí
Marratxinet
Pórtol
Sa Casa Blanca
Sant Jordi
C713
Sa Cabaneta
Son Ferriol
C715
Palma de Mallorca
PM-204
Festival Park
Pla de na Tesa
Son Amar
PM-27
Pont d'Inca
PM-19
Ses Llegitimes
S'Indioteria
C713
Es Molinar
Palmanyola
C711
PM-20
Coll d'en Rabassa
Lafiore Glass Factory
PM-114
Son Espanyol
Son Sardina
Portixol
Esporles
PM-112
S'Esgleieta
PM-111
PALMA
Ses Rogetes
PM-104
Establiments
Son Roca
PM-20
Fundació Pilar i Joan Miró
La Granja de Esporles
Son Comes
Sa Vileta
Coves de Gènova
Gènova
Cala Major
Son Vida
PM-1

N

THIEVES AND MONKEYS

Chopin and Sand came to Mallorca to escape the gossip of Paris, and hoping that the mild climate would improve Chopin's ill health. However, Chopin's piano failed to arrive, his health deteriorated and so did their relationship. Afterwards, Sand wrote an angry book, *A Winter in Mallorca*, in which she described the Mallorcans as 'thieves' and 'monkeys'. Despite this, and the fact that she was widely snubbed at the time, nowadays her book is proudly stocked all over the island.

CULTURE
La Cartoixa (The Charterhouse)

Visit the Carthusian monastery – the second most-visited site on the island (after Palma's cathedral) – to see the monk's cell where Frédéric Chopin and George Sand stayed, as well as the old pharmacy and an excellent museum of modern art including work by Picasso and Miró. There are regular recitals of Chopin's music and you can even buy a copy of Sand's book. ☎ (971) 612106 🕐 09.30–18.00 Mon–Sat, 10.00–13.00 Sun, Mar–Oct; 09.30–16.30 Mon–Sat, Nov & Feb, 09.30–15.00 Dec & Jan. Admission charge

La Granja de Esporles

If time permits, it's worth making a detour to see one of Mallorca's finest country houses, originally constructed by the Cistercians as a monastery, which has since been turned into a fascinating open-air museum of rural life and traditions. The best time to visit is during the 'folk fiesta' on Wednesday and Friday afternoons, when folk dancers perform in the courtyard and women in traditional

⬧ *The Charterhouse of Valldemossa has attracted visitors since Chopin's time*

OUT OF TOWN

🔺 *The Archduke's gazebo at Son Marroig*

costume give displays of lace-making and embroidery. There are free tastings of cheese and sausages, doughnuts and fig-cake, and the restaurant serves up typical Mallorcan fare. The tour of the house includes the family chapel, the medieval kitchens – and an incongruous 'torture chamber'. **ⓐ** Carretera Esporles– Puigpunyent, Km 2, Esporles **ⓣ** (971) 610032/ 619328/ 619299 **ⓦ** www.lagranja.net **ⓛ** 10.00–19.00 Apr–Oct, 10.00–18.00 Nov–Mar. Admission charge

Son Marroig

Perched high above the north coast between Valldemossa and Deià, with stunning sea views, this mansion was once the home of Mallorca's greatest admirer, the wealthy Austrian aristocrat and ecologist Archduke Luis Salvador. Known to the locals simply as 'S'Arxiduc', he spent the best part of his life here studying and recording Mallorcan wildlife and traditions. Today his house is open to the public, providing a fascinating insight into island life in bygone years. The garden contains a graceful white-marble rotunda where the Archduke would sit and contemplate the sea, the mountains and Sa Foradada – a remarkable rocky headland jutting out to sea with a massive hole at its centre. **ⓐ** Carretera Deià–Valldemossa **ⓦ** www.sonmarroig.com **ⓣ** (649) 913832 **ⓛ** 10.00–19.00 Mon–Sat (until 17.00 Nov–Mar). Admission charge

RETAIL THERAPY

There are plenty of souvenir, arts and handicraft shops in Valldemossa selling fine, handmade pottery, glass, jewellery, woodwork and table linen.

Blaumari This jam-packed shop sells everything from Lladro, lace and leatherware to *siurells* (see page 22) and replica Chopin pianos. **ⓐ** Pl. Cartoixa 1 **ⓣ** (971) 612461 **ⓛ** 10.00–18.00

Cals Tios Brightly coloured shoes, funky handbags and clothing and chunky costume jewellery, all made in Mallorca. **ⓐ** C/. Blanqueria 15c **ⓣ** (971) 612615 **ⓛ** 11.00–18.00 (winter); 11.00–20.00 (summer)

TAKING A BREAK

Don't leave Valldemossa without having tried the local delicacies – *coca de patates* (light, fluffy buns dusted in icing sugar) – washed down with a chilled *horchata de almendra* (almond milkshake).

Es Port £ Set in Valldemossa's isolated fishing village, this small bar and restaurant serves the freshest of fish and massive paellas. **ⓐ** Port de Valldemossa **ⓣ** (971) 616194 **ⓛ** 10.00–16.00 Nov–Apr; 13.00–15.30, 21.00–23.30 May–Oct

AFTER DARK

Restaurants

Sa Cartoixa ££ *Tumbet*, rabbit stew and paella are the specialities in this bustling café-restaurant right at the heart of the village. **ⓐ** Pl. Ramòn Llull 5 **ⓣ** (971) 616059 **ⓛ** 08.00–23.00 Tues–Sun

Ca'n Pedro ££ A large, atmospheric cellar restaurant on the edge of the village, serving hearty Mallorcan fare. Reservations essential. **ⓐ** C/. Arxiduc Lluis Salvador 25 **ⓣ** (971) 612170 **ⓛ** 13.00–15.30, 20.00–22.30 Tues–Sun am

ACCOMMODATION

Ca'n Mário ££ A simple budget hotel in the heart of the village, with just 16 rooms and a popular restaurant. **ⓐ** C/. de Uetam 8 **ⓣ** (971) 612122

◐ *Picturesque Valldemossa – a great place to escape from the city*

Hotel Valldemossa £££ A gorgeous luxury hotel with an outdoor pool and spa. All rooms have terraces, and most have great views. ⓐ Carretera Vieja de Valldemossa ⓣ (971) 612626 ⓦ www.valldemossahotel.com

DEIÀ

The artists' village of Deià is a tiny cluster of ochre-coloured houses in the shadow of the Teix Mountain, just a 25-minute drive north of Palma. It was put on the map by the author and poet Robert Graves, who lived here from the 1930s until his death in 1985. He is buried beneath a simple, hand-inscribed tombstone outside the church of Sant Joan Bautista at the top of the village. Deià has become a magnet for foreign artists over the last few decades, and the village is full of small art galleries, cafés and chic hotels. Having explored it, you may wish to take a drink or a meal at La Residencia (see page 127), which used to belong to Richard Branson – but be warned, it is very pricey. Centrally located, this 5-star hotel is set back off the main Deià road in beautiful terraced gardens.

SIGHTS & ATTRACTIONS
Cala de Deià
Just a 30-minute stroll from Deià, this tiny pebbly cove with its jagged cliffs and icy, clear waters is one of the hidden gems of Mallorca's north coast. There is even a ramshackle beach bar and a restaurant, Sa Caleta (see page 126), for refreshments.

CULTURE
Deià Archaeological Museum
Small, fascinating museum, worth visiting for the extremely

attractive conversion of an old mill and prehistoric finds from nearby caves. ⓐ Es Clot, Deià ⓣ (971) 639001 ⓦ www.sollernet.com/damarc ⓛ 17.00–19.00 Tues, Thur & Sun

⬤ *Celebrities past and present have chosen Deià as their Mediterranean hideaway*

LAFIORE GLASS FACTORY

Glass has been made on the island since Roman times and glass-making techniques have changed little since then. Here you can watch craftspeople at work in the glass-blowing workshop, before visiting the extensive shop next door where jugs, vases, drinking glasses and candleholders are the most popular buys. The Glass Factory is a great place both for wising up on the glass-blower's art and for picking up unique souvenirs.
ⓐ Carretera de Valldemossa, Km 11, S'Esgleieta ⓣ (971) 611800 ⓦ www.lafiore.com ⓛ 09.15–20.00 Mon–Fri, 09.15–13.00, 15.00–18.00 Sat

RETAIL THERAPY

Arte This artisan's workshop sells unusual pottery, glass and olivewood utensils. ⓐ Pl. de la Iglesia 2 ⓣ (971) 639126 ⓛ 11.00–13.30, 15.00–18.30 Mon–Sat am

Forn Deià Ca Na Margalida The village store is a fantastic one-stop shop for all your picnic needs. ⓐ C/. Arxiduc Lluis Salvador, Deià ⓛ 11.00–13.30, 16.00–20.00 Mon–Sat am

Taller de Joanna A tiny potter's workshop, crammed full of rustic dishes, tiles and door plaques. ⓐ Deià ⓣ (971) 639384 ⓛ 11.30–19.00 Mon–Sat

TAKING A BREAK

Sa Caleta £ Grilled squid, prawns and swordfish are the specialities in this beachside restaurant, perched high on the cliffs overlooking a picturesque cove. ⓐ Cala de Deià ⓣ (971) 639137 ⓛ 11.00–19.00

Xelini £ This cellar-style bar with stone floors serves a fantastic spread of tapas laid along a huge bar – everything from tortilla and shrimps to *sobrassada*, octopus and stuffed peppers. ⓐ C/. Arxiduc Lluis Salvador 19 ⓣ (971) 639139 ⓦ www.xelini.com ⓛ 12.30–24.00 Mon–Sat, closed mid-Nov–Christmas

AFTER DARK
Restaurants
El Olivo ££ Top-notch nouvelle cuisine in a converted oil-mill, attached to La Residencia hotel. ⓐ C/. Son Canals, s/n, Deià ⓣ (971) 639392 ⓛ 13.00–15.00, 20.00–23.00

Jaume ££ Mallorcan cuisine – *tumbet*, *sopes mallorquines*, *bacalao* (salt cod), etc – in a simple (yet stylish) dining room with a terrace overlooking the village and the valley. ⓐ C/. Arxiduc Lluis Salvador 22 ⓣ (971) 639029 ⓛ 13.00–16.00, 19.30–22.00 Tues–Sun, closed mid-Dec–mid-Feb

ACCOMMODATION
La Residencia £££ Mallorca's top country hotel, formerly owned by Richard Branson, with every imaginable home comfort. ⓐ C/. Son Canals, s/n ⓣ (971) 639011 ⓦ www.hotel-laresidencia.com

Villa Verde £££ A surprisingly affordable pension in the centre of Deià, with a beautiful terrace overlooking the village. Some rooms also have a terrace, with a view over the valley. ⓐ C/. Ramon Llull 19 ⓣ (971) 639037 ⓦ www.hostalvillaverde.com

Palma to Sóller

The old-fashioned, toytown train ride from Palma to Sóller is one of the highlights of any visit to Mallorca. The guards with their whistles, and the vintage carriages with their polished mahogany and brass panels, conjure up an image of a bygone age of travel. The 27 km (16 mile) journey takes about an hour. At the end of it all is a joyride down to the sea, in an antique tram imported from San Francisco.

GETTING THERE

The mountain train (❶ (971) 752051) is absolutely the best way to reach this part of Mallorca, but if you're feeling contrary there are three buses daily from Monday to Friday, and two buses daily at weekends, to Sóller (70 mins) and Port de Sóller (80 mins). By car Sóller is 28 km (17 miles) away, with the Port de Sóller another 4 km (2.5 miles) further on.

SÓLLER

The friendly market town of Sóller, nestling in the lush Valley of Oranges at the heart of the Serra de Tramuntana mountains, never fails to captivate its many visitors.

SIGHTS & ATTRACTIONS

Sóller had its heyday in the 19th century, with the production of olive oil and the export of oranges and lemons to the South of France directly from Port de Sóller. The influences of this flourishing trade

❶ The Sóller train spends a magic hour travelling through the mountains

can be seen today in the lovely manor houses and surrounding farmsteads whose façades show an elegance unusual for this type of rural building in Mallorca. Ca'n Prunera mansion, in Carrer Sa Lluna, and the Bank of Sóller, with its fancy wrought-ironwork, in Plaça Constitució, are just two examples. Today, Sóller is a delightful place to soak up the atmosphere of an authentic Mallorcan town, to enjoy a lazy lunch, or to potter about the traditional-style shops. And be sure to spend some time in the main square, Plaça Constitució – a pleasant place to sit and watch the trams, with their open-sided carriages, trundling past the church en route to picturesque Port de Sóller just a 30-minute ride away.

CULTURE

Museu del Casal de Cultura de Sóller

If you are interested in the history of the town, this delightful 18th-century manor house crammed with relics of old Sóller is worth a visit. ⓐ Casal de Cultura, C/. de Sa Mar 13 ⓣ (971) 631465 ⓦ www.sollernet.com/casal ⓛ 11.00–13.00, 17.00–20.00 Tues–Fri, 11.00–13.00 Sat, May–Sept; 11.00–13.00, 16.00–19.00 Tues–Fri, 11.00–13.00 Sat, Oct–Apr

RETAIL THERAPY

Sóller offers some of the island's best shopping outside Palma, with its numerous boutiques and craft shops. Stock up on fresh produce for a picnic on the beach at the daily covered market on Carrer Cristòfol Colom, or at the open-air market in Plaça del Mercat on Saturdays from 08.00–13.00. As in Palma, most shops are closed Saturday afternoons and on Sunday.

ⓞ *Sóller's architecture is surprisingly sophisticated for a small market town*

THE ORANGE BLIGHT

Situated in the broad, fertile Valle de los Naranjos (Valley of Oranges), Sóller is redolent of the 19th century, when its residents grew prosperous from the local fruit trade. However, in the 1860s the orange groves were struck by blight, and many of Sóller's citizens were forced to seek their fortunes elsewhere. Many emigrated to mainland Europe in search of work. When they returned they brought with them new ideas, including *Modernista* architecture.

Ben Calçat Small shoe manufacturer specialising in traditional Balearic footwear. ⓐ C/. Sa Lluna 74, Sóller ❶ (971) 632874 ❶ 09.00–20.30 Mon–Sat

Ca'n Oliver This fabric shop sells the distinctive Mallorca *roba de llengües* – durable cotton cloth with colourful stripey red, green or blue patterns. ⓐ C/. Lluna 25, Sóller ❶ (971) 638205 ❶ 09.00–13.00, 17.00–20.00 Mon–Fri, 09.00–13.00 Sat

Eugenio A treasure trove of Mallorcan pearls, fans and olive-wood souvenirs. ⓐ C/. Jerónimo Estades 11-A, Sóller ❶ (971) 630984 ❶ 10.30–13.00, 17.00–20.00 Mon–Fri, 10.30–13.00 Sat

TAKING A BREAK

The open-air cafés and tapas bars of Plaça Constitució are a great place to soak up the atmosphere of Sóller. Sample the local orange and lemon juice, freshly squeezed while you wait. For those with a sweet tooth, other local specialities include ice cream and pastries.

Bar Es Firo £ Try the hearty, country-style tapas here – the lamb with peppers and aubergines, fish in chilli and garlic, and snails with wild mushrooms are delicious. ⓐ Pl. Constitució 10b ⓣ (971) 630134 ⓛ 07.00–20.00

Sa Fàbrica de Gelats £ Children love to visit the small ice cream factory in the centre of town, well-known for its creamy ices made with the valley's famous oranges and lemons. ⓐ Avda. Cristòfol Colom 13 ⓣ (971) 631708 ⓛ 09.30–19.00

Es Planet £ Soak up the sun and the atmosphere on the pavement terrace of this popular café in the main square. It's one of the best places to try a glass of freshly squeezed orange or lemon juice. ⓐ Pl. Constitucio 3 ⓣ (971) 634570 ⓛ 08.30–20.30 Mon–Fri, 08.30–14.00 Sat

AFTER DARK
Restaurants
El Guia £ An old-fashioned restaurant serving staple Mallorcan cuisine. The *menú del día* is always excellent value. ⓐ C/. Castanyer 3 ⓣ (971) 630227 ⓛ 13.00–15.00, 20.00–22.00

Sa Cova ££ On Sóller's main square, this restaurant serves international cuisine as well as Mallorcan specialities, such as rabbit with garlic. ⓐ Pl. Constitució 7 ⓣ (971) 633222 ⓛ 12.30–16.30, 19.00–23.00 Mon–Sat, 12.30–16.30 Sun

ACCOMMODATION
L'Avenida Hotel £££ Opened in 2007, L'Avenida is a small, sumptuously comfortable hotel with stunning contemporary

design and a tranquil, leafy pool area. ⓐ Gran Via 9 ⓣ (971) 634075
ⓦ www.avenida-hotel.com ⓘ The hotel does not accommodate children

El Guia £££ A traditional hotel that makes an ideal base for
exploring the region. ⓐ C/. Castanyer 3 ⓣ (971) 630227
ⓦ www.sollernet.com/elguia ⓘ Closed Nov–Feb

Hotel Salvia £££ A beautifully renovated, 18th-century townhouse at
the heart of the town, with just six rooms and citrus-scented gardens
(and no children under 14). ⓐ C/. de la Palma 18 ⓣ (971) 634936
ⓦ www.hotelsalvia.com ⓘ Closed Nov–Mar

PORT DE SÓLLER

The Orange Express trams from Sóller to its port leave every half
hour (07.00–20.00) from the station and the main square, passing
through orchards of citrus fruit on their way down to the sea. The
two beaches at Port de Sóller are the only sandy ones along the
entire northern coast until Cala Sant Vicenç to the north. The main
beach runs beside the tramway. The second beach – Platja d'en Repic
– fronts an attractive pedestrian promenade. Both have sun beds,
parasols and pedalos for hire.

SIGHTS & ATTRACTIONS
Boat trips
Some of the finest views of Port de Sóller and the Serra de Tramuntana
mountains beyond can only be seen from the sea. Hop on a pleasure
cruise to admire the dramatic coastline, and remember your camera!

● *Fishing nets are laid out to dry in Port de Sóller*

CULTURE

Museu de la Mar

This small museum in the fishermen's quarter of Port de Sóller tells the fascinating history of the people of Sóller. ⓐ Oratori de Santa Caterina d'Alexandria ⓣ (971) 630200 ⓦ www.a-soller.tiscalibiz.com/ museudelamar ⓛ 10.00–14.00, 17.00–20.00 Tues–Sat, 10.00–14.00 Sun, June–Sept; 10.00–13.30, 15.00–18.00 Tues–Sat, 10.00–14.00 Sun, Oct–May

AFTER DARK
Restaurants
Es Faro ££ Enjoy 'The Lighthouse's' delicious fish dishes, served on a terrace high above the port, and drink in the spectacular view. ⓐ Carretera Faro, Cap Gros de Muleta ⓣ (971) 633752 ⓛ 12.30–16.00, 19.00–23.00 Wed–Mon

⬇ *Port de Sóller has a thriving nightlife*

● *Mallorcan soup served in a bread dish*

Lua ££ A tiny, chic restaurant in the fishermen's quarter, perched high above the port, with exceptional views, fine wines and the freshest of fish. ⓐ C/. Santa Catalina 1 ❶ (971) 634745 ● 12.30–15.30, 19.00–22.00 Tues–Sun

ACCOMMODATION

Aimia ££ Located just one street back from the beach, everything about this chic modern hotel is designed for comfort and relaxation. ⓐ C/. Santa Maria del Camí 1 ❶ (971) 631200 Ⓦ www.aimiahotel.com ❶ Closed Nov–Jan

Espléndido Hotel ££ An impressive refurbishment of a faded seafront hotel from the design-conscious Swedish duo behind the Hotel Portixol in Palma. As well as two pools and a spa, the hotel has its own private beach. ⓐ C/. Es Traves 5 ❶ (971) 633 019 Ⓦ www.esplendidohotel.com

SERRA DE TRAMUNTANA

Only a 15-minute drive from Sóller is the rugged Serra de Tramuntana, with excellent hiking and some attractive little villages. Visible from all over Mallorca, the 'Mountains of the North Wind' stretch along the entire northwest coast and provide some of the island's most dramatic scenery. In winter they act as a buffer, shielding the central plain from the fierce *tramuntana* wind and absorbing much of the island's rain and snow. In summer, they provide a cool retreat from the heat of Palma and the frenetic resorts of the south.

Alfàbia

Just a couple of kilometres from Sóller, the cool, fragrant gardens of Alfàbia evoke the period when Mallorca was under Moorish rule. With shaded walkways and gently splashing fountains, it is an ideal spot to escape the sun. ❸ Carretera Palma–Sóller, Km 17 (at the entrance to the Sóller tunnel) ❶ (971) 613123 Ⓦ www.jardinesdealfabia.com Ⓛ 09.30–18.30 Mon–Fri, 09.30– 13.00 Sat, May–Oct; 09.30–17.30 Mon–Fri, 09.30–13.00 Sat, Nov–Apr. Admission charge

Bunyola

The train rattles through Palma's poorer suburbs and out onto the pancake-flat plain, passing almond and orange groves before climbing to the hill village of Bunyola. If you want to break your journey, you can get off here to explore this pretty village and to visit the Tunel factory, where many of Mallorca's herb-based liqueurs are made. Be sure to try the *palo*, a sweet, carob-based liqueur. ❸ C/. Vinyetes, Bunyola

Fornalutx

Fornalutx claims to be the most beautiful village in all Spain, set in a valley of citrus groves with Puig Major, the highest mountain on the island, as its backdrop. Its honey-coloured houses and steep cobbled streets dotted with café terraces are a joy.

AFTER DARK
Restaurants
Café Med ££ A small restaurant just off the main square in Fornalutx, serving sophisticated international cuisine in simple, rustic surroundings. ⓐ C/. sa Plaça 7, Fornalutx ❶ (971) 630900 ❶ 19.30–22.00 Sun–Fri, closed Nov–mid-Feb

Ses Porxeres ££ Located inside a high-ceilinged barn beside the gardens of Alfàbia, this restaurant is renowned for its game dishes. ⓐ Carretera Palma-Sóller (at the entrance to the Sóller tunnel), Alfàbia ❶ (971) 613762 ❶ 13.30–15.30, 20.30–23.30 Tues–Sat, 13.30–15.30 Sun

Entertainment
Son Amar Mallorca's top nightspot, with spectacular live cabaret, near Bunyola. ⓐ Carretera de Sóller, Km 10, Bunyola ❶ (971) 617533 ⓦ www.sonamar.com

ACCOMMODATION
Ca'n Reus ££ A charming, small hotel, popular with walkers, with nine rooms and a pretty garden, pool and terrace overlooking citrus groves and the mountains. ⓐ C/. de l'Auba 26, Fornalutx ❶ (971) 631174 ⓦ www.canreushotel.com

---

▶ *Old Palma offers a small maze of medieval streets*

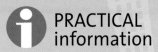

PRACTICAL
information

Directory

GETTING THERE

Most major tour operators offer package holidays to the Balearics, and there are often good last-minute deals to be had. A number of no-frills airlines also serve the island. The Palma Town Council website may help your holiday planning ⓦ www.palmademallorca.es

By air

Palma de Mallorca Airport (ⓣ (971) 789000) is 8 km (5 miles) southeast of the city centre. Frequent buses run between the airport and Passeig Marítim (number 1, every 15 minutes from 07.00 to 21.00). Iberia, the Spanish national airline, operates scheduled flights from mainland Spain and Europe, although there are charter and no-frills options, too. Flying from the UK takes about two hours. Information and reservations can be made through the websites of leading airlines and tour operators.

Air Berlin ⓣ (UK) 0870 738 8880, (Spain) (902) 320737
ⓦ www.airberlin.com

Air Europa ⓣ (UK) 0870 777 7709, (Palma) (971) 221686
ⓦ www.aireuropa.com

BMI ⓣ (UK) 0870 607 0555, (Spain) (902) 100737 ⓦ www.flybmi.com

British Airways ⓣ (UK) 0870 850 9850, (Spain) (902) 111333
ⓦ www.britishairways.com

British Midland ⓣ (UK) 0870 607 0555, (Spain) (902) 999262
ⓦ www.britishmidland.com

EasyJet ⓣ (UK) 0871 244 2366, (Palma) (971) 490307
ⓦ www.easyjet.com

First Choice ⓣ (UK) 0870 850 3999, (Palma) (971) 787947
ⓦ www.firstchoice.co.uk

▲ *Palma de Mallorca Airport is modern and hi-tech*

Iberia ❶ (UK) 0870 609 0500, (Palma) (971) 789980
Ⓦ www.iberia.com
Ryanair ❶ (UK) 0871 246 0000 Ⓦ www.ryanair.com
Thomas Cook ❶ (UK) 0870 243 0416
Ⓦ www.thomascookairlines.co.uk
Thomsonfly ❶ (UK) 0870 190 0737, (Spain) (914) 141481
Ⓦ www.thomsonfly.com

Visitors from the USA and other continents need to take a connecting flight from the UK or other European airport. Visitors from elsewhere in Europe should travel via their nearest major city, all of which have plane connections to Palma or Barcelona, which has regular ferries to Palma (see page 144).

Many people are aware that air travel emits CO_2, which contributes to climate change. You may be interested in the possibility of lessening the environmental impact of your flight through Climate Care, which offsets your CO_2 emissions by funding environmental projects around the world. Visit Ⓦ www.climatecare.org

By rail

It takes just 15 hours by train from London via the Channel Tunnel and Paris to Barcelona, from where there are regular ferries to Palma. Contact Rail Europe for further information. The monthly Thomas Cook European Rail Timetable has up-to-date schedules for European international and national train and ferry services.

Rail Europe Ⓦ www.raileurope.com

Thomas Cook European Rail Timetable Ⓣ (UK) 01733 416477; (USA) 1 800 322 3834 Ⓦ www.thomascookpublishing.com

By road

The usual route by car involves driving down through France and across the Pyrénées to Barcelona (allow not less than two days), where you can catch the daily car ferry. The journey from London to Barcelona by coach takes around 26 hours. Contact Eurolines for further information.

Eurolines Ⓣ (UK) 0870 514 3219 Ⓦ www.eurolines.com

By water

There are regular ferry services connecting Palma to Barcelona, Valencia and Dénia on the Spanish mainland, as well as to the Balearic Islands of Menorca and Ibiza. Contact the operators Trasmediterránea and Balearia for further information.

Balearia Ⓦ www.balearia.com
Trasmediterránea Ⓦ www.trasmediterranea.com

ENTRY FORMALITIES

Citizens of EU countries, USA, Canada, Australia, New Zealand and Japan who hold valid passports do not need a visa to visit Spain for less than 90 days. Other visitors should check with their nearest Spanish consulate.

Visitors to Mallorca from within the EU are entitled to bring their personal effects and goods for personal consumption and not for resale, up to a total of 800 cigarettes and ten litres of spirits. Duty-free limits for those entering from outside the EU are 200 cigarettes (or 100 cigarillos or 50 cigars or 250g of tobacco), one litre of spirits (or two litres of fortified wines or sparkling wine) and two litres of wine.

MONEY

Spain's currency is the euro, with notes issued in denominations of 5, 10, 20, 50, 100, 200 and 500 euros, and coins of 1 and 2 euros and also 1, 2, 5, 10, 20 and 50 cents. Credit cards are widely used in Palma (especially American Express, Visa and MasterCard), and you should always carry ID that proves you're the card-holder. It's a good idea to carry cash to use in shops, bars and cafés, and to check the payment methods available before you order a meal or run up a bar bill. If you do get caught short, there are numerous bureaux de change in Palma and most UK banks' cash cards can be used to obtain cash in local currency from some ATMs, although the commission charged can be expensive.

HEALTH, SAFETY & CRIME

The water in Palma is generally safe to drink, although it is heavily chlorinated and not to everyone's taste. Bottled water is cheap to buy and is preferable, either still (*agua sin gas*) or carbonated (*agua con gas*).

Thanks to a reciprocal healthcare agreement, nationals of EU countries and some other countries can get reduced-price, sometimes free, medical treatment in Spain on presentation of a valid European Health Insurance Card (EHIC). This card gives access to state-provided medical treatment only. Apply online for an EHIC at Ⓦ www.dh.gov.uk/travellers and allow at least two–three weeks to receive the card. Private medical insurance is essential for all non-EU visitors. Dental treatment is not available free of charge, as Mallorcan dental practices are private, and should be covered by private medical insurance.

The biggest health hazards for visitors are sunstroke, dehydration and alcoholic over-indulgence. People who are not used to the sun burn easily, and children are especially vulnerable. It is a good idea to cover up with a strong sunblock, to wear a hat and to keep out of the midday sun by taking a siesta in the shade. Remember also to drink alcohol in moderation and plenty of water.

If you need to consult a doctor (*médico*) or a dentist (*dentista*), ask for help at your hotel reception. Prescription and non-prescription medicines are available from pharmacies (*farmàcias*), indicated by a large green cross, and there is an extensive network of health centres (*centres de salut*), which provide medical advice. A list of pharmacies open out of hours is shown in all pharmacy windows. Alternatively, dial ☎ 11888 for information on all-night pharmacies. (For information on medical emergencies, see page 154.)

Crime rates are low in Palma, although it is advisable to take commonsense precautions against petty crime (see page 50). If you need a police station, ask for *la comisaría*.

OPENING HOURS

Most shops are open Monday to Friday 09.00–13.00 and 16.30–20.00 (or later in summer months), and on Saturday mornings. The siesta is still a time-honoured custom in Palma and very necessary during the hot summer months if you intend to keep going into the small hours of the morning like the locals. The siesta generally runs from 13.30 to as late as 17.00, although hypermarkets and department stores remain open, as do many shops in the coastal resorts. Restaurants don't normally start serving dinner until 20.00 and are at their busiest around 23.00, which is when the discos and clubs start to fill up, although their special shows do not normally begin until 01.00 or so.

Banks are generally open from Monday to Thursday 08.30–14.30, and Fridays until 14.00. Most post offices open from Monday to Friday from 09.30–13.00 and 16.00–19.00, and Saturday mornings, but Palma's main post office in Carrer de Constitució is open Monday to Friday from 08.30–20.30 and Saturdays from 09.30–14.00. Museum opening times vary. Most are open at least 10.00–13.00 and 16.00–18.00, and some have extended hours during summer. Many close for at least one day a week, usually Monday, but occasionally Sunday.

TOILETS

Public toilets are still not widespread and it is no longer quite so common to wander into a bar merely to use their *servicios* without buying something. Indeed, many bars have notices prohibiting just that – you will see signs saying *Aseos reservados para clients* (lavatories reserved for clients only). Public toilets can be found in hypermarkets, supermarkets, department stores and underground car parks. However, they are unlikely to have paper. There are good facilities in all the major museums and galleries.

CHILDREN

Children are doted on in Palma. Restaurants, cafés and even bars will generally be happy to cater for them, and the preference for al fresco dining from April to October removes any concerns about smoky air and fidgeting.

If you need to hire a car seat for a child, double-check availability when making the booking. Nappies, baby food and formula milk can be bought in supermarkets in Palma, but if you have a preferred brand take a supply with you. Some hotels offer a room-listening service for the evenings. Ask your reception also about *canguros* (professional baby-sitters) and local *guarderías* (crèches).

There is no shortage of sights and activities that are guaranteed to keep the kids entertained. It's hard to go wrong with a bit of child-friendly transport, so why not take a boat trip around Palma Bay, from Passeig Marítim (see page 80). Some boats have glass bottoms so you can see the fish. A hop-on-hop-off bus tour (see page 56) is always a hoot, and no doubt you'll enjoy a trundle in an open-top bus yourself as it tours the city sights. Little girls in particular will love exploring Palma's Old Town by horse and carriage (a *galera*, see page 56).

If your little pixies need to expend some energy, why not visit the city's parks? The playground at the eastern end of Parc de la Mar (see page 62) is especially good for toddlers. Not surprisingly, the whole area has loads of beach and water sports options. The fine sandy beaches at Cala Major, Portals Nous, Palmanova and Magaluf are all within easy reach of the city to the west, or head east to the Playa de Palma, 7 km (4 miles) of golden sandy bliss stretching from Ca'n Pastilla to S'Arenal. Each beach offers various water sports, from pedalo rides to more energetic activities for teenagers, such as windsurfing, canoeing and snorkelling.

▼ *A boat trip is a great treat for the kids*

Marineland, Costa d'En Blanes (see page 104) is a fantastic water park with displays of performing dolphins, sea lions and parrots, while Aqualand S'Arenal and Aqualand Magaluf (see page 100) focus on fantastic family fun. Indeed, the new Palma Aquarium (see page 104) focuses on *fishy*, fantastic, family fun.

Kids love a bit of a splash-fest, and there are plenty on offer at **Western Water Park** (ⓐ Carretera Cala Figuera Sa Porrasa 12–22, Magaluf ⓣ (971) 131203 ⓦ www.westernpark.com), where there are also horse-riding shows, cowboy capers and can-can dancers. The area's newest attraction for children is **House of Katmandu** (ⓐ Avda. Pedro Vaqer Ramis 9, Magaluf ⓣ (971) 134660 ⓦ www.houseofkatmandu.com), an adventure complex based in – wait for it – an upside-down house.

COMMUNICATIONS
Internet
There are cybercafés all over the city, and hotels and cafés are getting all Wi-Fi'd up. Three of the best cybercafés are:
Blond Café ⓐ Pl. Salvador Coll 10 ⓣ (971) 728 588 ⓦ www.blondcafé.com ⓛ 09.00–23.00 Mon–Sat
CyberCentral ⓐ C/. Soledat 4 ⓣ (971) 712 927 ⓛ 09.30–14.00, 16.00–20.00 Mon–Fri, 14.00–16.00 Sat
Manamú Café ⓐ C/. Concepció 5 ⓣ (971) 729294 ⓛ 09.00–01.30 Mon–Fri, 19.00–02.00 Sat

Phone
Public phones are easy to use. Most take coins, phone cards and credit cards and they have instructions for use in English: basically lift the receiver, insert payment and dial the number. Phone cards can be purchased from post offices and many other shops. Mallorca

TELEPHONING PALMA

All telephone numbers in the Balearic Islands begin with (971) followed by a six-digit number. To call them from abroad, dial your international access code (00 in most countries), followed by the code for Spain (34), and then the number beginning with 971. The Mallorcan Yellow Pages (Páginas Amarillas) has a very comprehensive index in English. Its centre pages contain detailed street plans of Palma and other towns.

TELEPHONING ABROAD

To phone abroad from Palma, dial the international access code (00), followed by the relevant country code: UK 44, USA and Canada 1, Australia 61, New Zealand 64, Republic of Ireland 353, South Africa 27, then the local code (minus the initial 0, if there is one) and finally the number you want.

has a good mobile phone network, although you may have problems getting a signal in parts of the interior. If you plan to use your mobile abroad, check with your service provider that you will be able to access the relevant networks.

Calls to the operator ⓘ 1002
International enquiries ⓘ 11825
National enquiries ⓘ 11818

Post

The Mallorcan post is moderately efficient. The bright yellow post offices and post boxes are easy to spot, and stamps (*sellos*) are available from any tobacconist or at the post office. The main post

office in Palma is in Carrer de Constitució 6 (**☏** (971) 228882), and is
open Mon–Fri 08.30–20.30 Mon–Fri, and Sat morning.

ELECTRICITY

Electricity is supplied at 220–240 volts. Spanish plugs are of the
two-pin round plug variety, so an adapter will be required for
British and non-Continental appliances. US and other visitors
with 110-volt appliances will need to use a voltage transformer,
too. If you are considering buying electrical appliances to take
home, always check that they will work in your home country
before you buy.

TRAVELLERS WITH DISABILITIES

Although the authorities are working hard to improve facilities for
visitors with disabilities, much still remains to be done. Check with
your travel company on the hotels that provide facilities for the
disabled. All radio taxi companies offer modified taxis to accommodate
wheelchairs, but they need to be booked in advance. For further
information, contact:

Asprom Mallorca's main association for people with disabilities.
ⓐ C/. Pascual Ribot 6a **☏** (971) 289052
Disabled Persons Transport Advisory Committee (UK)
ⓦ www.dptac.gov.uk/door-to-door
SATH (Society for Accessible Travel & Hospitality) A group advising
US-based travellers with disabilities. **ⓐ** 347 Fifth Ave, Suite 610,
New York, NY 10016 **☏** (212) 447 7284 **ⓦ** www.sath.org

TOURIST INFORMATION

Palma's Tourist Information Offices (*Oficines d'Informació Turística*)
are useful for maps, attractions and event information, and any

other queries you have about the city. Two are located in the city centre and there is also one in arrivals at the airport:

OIT Municipal de Palma @ Passeig des Born 27 ☎ (971) 729634
🕐 09.00–20.00

OIT Municipal de Palma @ Pl. d'Espanya ☎ (971) 92758
🕐 09.00–20.00 ℹ️ Enquiries in person only.

OIT Aeroport ☎ (971) 789556.

The regional tourist office website is 🌐 www.infomallorca.net

BACKGROUND READING

Jogging around Majorca by Gordon West. A light-hearted account of island travels in the 1920s.

Problem at Pollensa Bay by Agatha Christie. A romantic, short thriller set in the north coast resort of Pollença.

Wild Olives by William Robert Graves. Portraits of daily life in Mallorca with the English poet, novelist and former Deià resident, Robert Graves, written by his son.

Our Man in Majorca by Tom Crichton. An entertaining account of life as a tour rep in the 1960s.

Snowball Oranges and *Mañana Mañana* by Peter Kerr. An account of a Scottish family moving to Mallorca to run an orange farm, and its sequel, adjusting to the slow pace of island life.

Emergencies

EMERGENCY NUMBERS

The following are handy numbers in the event of an emergency:

Emergency Coordination Centre ☎ 112 (dial this number in any type of emergency. They speak English and will alert the relevant service).

Police (*Policía Nacional*, for theft) ☎ 091 (Palma); 112 (rest of island)

City Police (*Policía Municipal*, for traffic accidents) ☎ 092 (Palma); 112 (rest of island)

Fire (*Bomberos*) ☎ 080 (Palma); 085 (rest of the island)

Ambulance (*Ambulància*) ☎ 112

General medical emergencies ☎ 061

Private medical assistance (24 hour) ☎ 900 722222

MEDICAL SERVICES

Should you become ill, lists of local doctors, dentists and hospitals can be found in telephone directories, local newspapers or by contacting your consulate, who have lists of English-speaking practitioners. Alternatively, ask your hotel reception to help, or, in a real emergency, dial 112. If you have a valid European Health Insurance Card (EHIC, see page 146), you should ensure that the doctor is part of the Spanish healthcare system, as the card only covers state-provided medical treatment. Be forewarned; it may not cover all the things you may expect to receive free of charge. If you are seen at a private clinic, you will need to pay on the spot and be reimbursed by your insurance company at a later date.

In an emergency, go to the Outpatient emergency department of Hospital Son Dureta, the university hospital, which is located on the outskirts of the city, just north of Castell de Bellver.

Hospital Son Dureta ⓐ C/. Andrea Dòria 55 ☎ (971) 175000
ⓦ www.hsd.es ⓝ Bus: 4, 5

POLICE

The city police or *Policia Municipal* wear blue and control traffic, while the *Policia Nacional* wear brown and uphold law and order. Police stations are open 24 hours a day.

Policia Municipal 🖂 C/. de Sant Ferran, Palma 📞 (971) 225500 (also for lost property)

Policia Nacional 🖂 C/. de Ruiz Alda 8, Palma 📞 (971) 225200

EMBASSIES AND CONSULATES

British Consulate 🖂 Avda. Plaça Major 3D, Palma 📞 (971) 712085
United States 🖂 C/. Porto Pi, 8, Palma 📞 (971) 403707
Canadian 🖂 Pl. de Catalunya 9, Barcelona 📞 (93) 4127236
Australian 🖂 Plaza del Descubridor Diego de Ordas 3, Madrid 📞 (91) 3536600
New Zealand 🖂 3rd floor, Plaza de La Lealtad 2, Madrid 📞 (91) 5230226
South African 🖂 Parc Empresarial Mas Blau II, Alta Ribagorza 6–8, Prat de Llobregat, Barcelona 📞 935 069100

EMERGENCY PHRASES

Help!	**Fire!**	**Stop!**
¡Socorro!	¡Fuego!	¡Stop!
¡Sawkoro!	*¡Fwegoh!*	*¡Stop!*

Call an ambulance/a doctor/the police/the fire service!
¡Llame a una ambulancia/un médico/la policía/a los bomberos!
¡Lliame a oona amboolanthea/oon meydico/la poleytheea/ a lohs bombehrohs!

WHAT'S IN YOUR GUIDEBOOK?

Independent authors Impartial up-to-date information from our travel experts who meticulously source local knowledge.

Experience Thomas Cook's 165 years in the travel industry and guidebook publishing enriches every word with expertise you can trust.

Travel know-how Contributions by thousands of staff around the globe, each one living and breathing travel.

Editors Travel-publishing professionals, pulling everything together to craft a perfect blend of words, pictures, maps and design.

You, the traveller We deliver a practical, no-nonsense approach to information, geared to how you really use it.

SPOTTED YOUR NEXT CITY BREAK?

Then these lightweight CitySpots pocket guides will have you in the know in no time, wherever you're heading. Covering over 80 cities worldwide, they're packed with detail on the most important urban attractions from shopping and sights to non-stop nightlife; knocking spots off chunkier, clunkier versions.

Aarhus	Genoa	Paris
Amsterdam	Glasgow	Prague
Antwerp	Gothenburg	Porto
Athens	Granada	Reykjavik
Bangkok	Hamburg	Riga
Barcelona	Hanover	Rome
Belfast	Helsinki	Rotterdam
Belgrade	Hong Kong	Salzburg
Berlin	Istanbul	Sarajevo
Bilbao	Kiev	Seville
Bologna	Krakow	Singapore
Bordeaux	Kuala Lumpur	Sofia
Bratislava	Leipzig	Stockholm
Bruges	Lille	Strasbourg
Brussels	Lisbon	St Petersburg
Bucharest	Ljubljana	Tallinn
Budapest	London	Tirana
Cairo	Los Angeles	Tokyo
Cape Town	Lyon	Toulouse
Cardiff	Madrid	Turin
Cologne	Marrakech	Valencia
Copenhagen	Marseilles	Venice
Cork	Milan	Verona
Dubai	Monte Carlo	Vienna
Dublin	Moscow	Vilnius
Dubrovnik	Munich	Warsaw
Düsseldorf	Naples	Zagreb
Edinburgh	New York	Zurich
Florence	Nice	
Frankfurt	Oslo	
Gdansk	Palermo	
Geneva	Palma	

Available from all good bookshops, your local Thomas Cook travel store or browse and buy on-line at www.thomascookpublishing.com

Thomas Cook Publishing

Editorial/project management: Lisa Plumridge with Laetitia Clapton
Copy editor: Paul Hines
Layout/DTP: Pat Hinsley & Alison Rayner
Proofreader: Yvonne Bergman

The publishers would like to thank the following for supplying their copyright photographs for this book: A1 Pix, pages 7, 64, 105, 129, 130, 136–7 & 149; BigStockPhoto.com (Cornel Achirei, pages 8 & 21; Jeff Gynane, page 143; Robert Taylor, page 16; Aleksey Trefilov, page 141; Holger Wulschlaeger, page 25); Dreamstime.com (Cornel Achirei, pages 54–5; Mark Bond, page 78; Harryfn, page 87; Nicky Jacobs, page 37; Tatiana Krivoshey, page 101; Anne-Britt Svinnset, pages 46 & 135); Iberimage, pages 10 & 45; iStockphoto.com (Wolfgang Eichentopf, page 115; Klaas Lingbeek van Kranen, page 5; Mark Mallinder, page 30); Palau Sa Font Hotel, page 34; SXC.hu (Katarzyna Bienias, page 138; Bodhy, page 119; Caroline Hoos, page 40); Teresa Fisher, all others.

Send your thoughts to
books@thomascook.com

- **Found a great bar, club, shop or must-see sight that we don't feature?**
- **Like to tip us off about any information that needs a little updating?**
- **Want to tell us what you love about this handy little guidebook and more importantly how we can make it even handier?**

Then here's your chance to tell all! Send us ideas, discoveries and recommendations today and then look out for your valuable input in the next edition of this title.

Email the above address (stating the title) or write to: CitySpots Project Editor, Thomas Cook Publishing, PO Box 227, Coningsby Road, Peterborough PE3 8SB, UK.